Education and Morality in India

D. Tejeswara Rao

2000
Kaveri Books
New Delhi - 110 002

First Published in 2000

ISBN: 81-7479-032-2

Published by: Rakesh Goel
Kaveri Books
4697/5-21 A, Ansari Road,
New Delhi-110002 (India).
Tel.: 3288140 Fax : 011-7198902
e-mail : kaveri books @ vsnl.com

Laser Typeset by: Niti Graphics, Delhi- 110035.

Printed at: Chawla Offset Printers, Delhi-110052.

PRINTED IN INDIA

Acknowledgements

I am thankful to my former teachers in the Department of Philosophy & Religious Studies, Andhra University, Waltair, Prof. V. Gopalakrishnayya, Prof. S. Satyanarayana, Prof. M.V. Krishnayya, Prof. George Victor, Prof. V.V. S. Saibaba, Prof. Y.V. Satyanarayana, and Prof. T. Cristhanandan.

I am thankful to the former Vice-Chancellor, Dr. M. Gopala Krishna Reddy, Andhra University and Principal of Arts and Commerce Colleges and the concerned authorities of the University for their help and encouragement.

It is my duty to express my heartful thanks to my uncle, P. Ramaswamy, Rtd. Dy. Collector, Srikakulam; to my brother K. Madhava Rao, Zonal Marketing Manager, Coromandel Fertilisers Ltd., Visakhapatnam; and to my brother D. Annaji Rao, Branch Manager, Sri Visakha Grameena Bank, Ponduru. In the same way I am grateful to my family members whose encouragement inspired me in pursuit of my research work.

I will always remember the Dr. V. S. K. Memorial Library and the Staff of the Library, Andhra University, Waltair; I also thankful to my friend S. Syam Sundara Reddy, Research Scholar in our Department who inspired me and for his encouragement, and my friends in the University who assisted to me at final stage of work.

Last but not least, my heartful thanks to D. Joga Rao, S.V. G. Bank, Amadalavalasa.

D. Tejeswara Rao

Contents

Introduction

The fundamental aim of this study is to make a study of the place that is being given to morality in Indian education in its major periods and with that background to show how modern education is faces moral problems in its institutions and to find out some causes and remedies for such problems. Education was mainly intended to mould the moral conduct of the youth but it is deteriorating from that aim. It is an open fact that, modern education is failing in its duty to have any noteworthy influence, in guiding and controlling the behaviour of its students. Actually classrooms are the real places where the destiny of the country is decided. Education has turned to be basically, a process of imparting some general and specific knowledge and skills in different fields and to help the youth earn a livelyhood and lead a common life without any exitement and fulfilment. Of course, at present, there is no guarantee of securing proper or any jobs, even with a high ranked degrees. Educational institutions are not actually feeling responsible for the present and future lives of their students, in the campus and out of it respectively. They became mechanical in their routine work, treating its youth as products of their machinery. Youth coming out of such institutions are baffelled, not aware of how to behave properly in the society not having definite values or ideals to lead their future life, to make it meaningful and worth living.

Modern Educational Institutions are facing more and more moral problems day by day and the intensity of them is also increasing. Another fact in this is the number and intensity of the problem in an ascending order from the lower levels to the higher levels of education. Actually this must be in a descending order, as the child grows in age and intelligence and learns the ways of moral behaviour. Students are not the only misbehaved persons in the educational institutions but teachers and administrators are also involved in such actions. Now-a-day such actions are being considered as a matter of fact and no serious action or any remedial measure are levied. Even Governments are showing a negligent view regarding such issues and this is encouraging in increasing the incidents.

Class-rooms and the campuses became the main places to encourage such immorality in the students. Teacher-student interactions in dealing with subject-matter as a medium, is the actual situation where students should be helped to develop their moral conduct. It is an opportunity to the teacher where he can exercise his abilities and responsibilities to the maximum, keeping an open heart to mould the students with desirable and socially accepted norms and Standards in a suitable way. He is the right person to check them by using his own personality and the approved methods. Priority must be given to teaching of values, especially moral values when compared to other subjects, and every subject must be used, when the opportunity arises, to impart moral values. The teacher must inculcate in the students moral values and behaviour. Administrators are another important persons to help to mould the moral behaviour of the students by this right moral ways of running the institution, and by this personal examples. They are the persons who are responsible for creating a moral atmosphere in the institution and maintaining it at any cost for the moral development of the youth.

Government and political parties are getting involved in the conduct of the educational institutions by influencing the students, teachers, as well as, the administrators, for their personal gains. Their part should be to help to maintain the academic and moral excellence of the educational institutions to uplift the country, but not to destroy it.

In this work, the education of India is considered from a broader perspective, with its different aims and activities. The moral aspect of education is not shown separately, picking it out from its surroundings, but as part and parcel of the different educational activities and individuals involved in this endeavour. Educational activities like aims, content of education, methods of teaching, system of education, teacher, student and their interrelations, etc., are taken into consideration, to bring to light the importance that has been given in moulding the moral lives of the students.

The intension of this work is to highlight the problems that are being faced by modern Indian education from the immoral or indisciplinary behaviour of the youth, in the educational institutions, especially at the higher level colleges and universities. And pains have been taken to show the causes for such moral crisis in the portals of educational institutions. Teachers and administrators have also been taken into consideration here as involved in creating such problems. What facts are gathered here, point to existing deeper and unseen influences as causes for such incidents of behaviour. And in a broader way, light is thrown in proposing some fundamental remedies for such problems. It was felt during this work that studying both the causes and remedial measures require a still deeper study of the problem, not only in a historical and documentary method, which are used here in this work, as well as more extensive practical and experimental methods that must be used in a scientific way, studying the problems directly with observation and questionaries in different problem areas.

The study has been divided into six chapters, depending on the major periods of Indian education, and according to convenience subdivided, based on types of education held by different people. The first chapter, 'Morality and Education' is intended to be an introductory one to show the relation and importance of 'morality' to education in general. In this, 'morality' as a moral conduct has been explained with its meaning and nature and functions in a basic way. And in the same lines 'education' has been considered. Next the importance and significance of education has been tackled, keeping as its basis, development of the moral behaviour of youth as its fundamental aim.

The second chapter, 'Education in Traditional India', is subdivided into two sections—Hindu Educational Practices' and

'Buddhist Educational Practices'. In these two sections, it has been tried to show, as historical facts, the place of morality in their respective educational practices. Areas like aims, content, methods of teaching, system of education, student and teacher modes of behaviour, are taken into consideration, to study the moral aspect and how much of importance they prescribed and their educational practices as part and parcel of it, rather than shown only that aspect separately.

The third chapter is devoted to the historical study of the 'Education in Medieval India', and for convenience, it is divided into two sections, 'Muslim Education' and 'Hindu Education'. In this chapter also the same procedure as in the second chapter, has been followed.

The fourth chapter, 'Education in Modern India', is divided into two sections as 'Education in British India' and 'Education in Post-Independence India'. This chapter is again subdivided into three parts: Morality and Education at the primary level; Morality and Education at the Secondary level; and Morality and Education at the Higher level. Here the writer has taken pains, to show how the Government Committees and Commissions, realising the deteriorating conditions of moral side of education, insisted on the urgent need of it in the modern education, at all the levels, to make it part of the curriculum. But implementation measures have not been taken up, and the present moral crisis is the result of neglecting such an important issue. Here also, as in the above two chapters, pains have been taken to reveal the position of moral values in all the main aims and activities. In this chapter, a special interest has been exercised to show the educational activities from the moral point of view only unlike the other chapters. Here a decline in the stress of imparting moral values and moulding character is revealed, and these aims are undermined by the stress on the material values in modern education.

The fifth chapter is mainly devoted to 'Immorality and Modern Indian Education with special reference to Higher Education: Some Causes and Remedies'. According to convenience this chapter has been divided into three sections-'Misbehaviour of the Students'; Misbehaviour of Teachers' and 'Misbehaviour of Administrators'. And these sections have been dealt under three sub-headings-

Moral problems, causes of the moral problems and some remedial measures. Stress is laid on the higher educational institutions, especially universities, to show the intensity of the problem and the deteriorating conditions of modern education from its fundamental moral aim. Causes and remedial measures for such immoral crisis has been pointed out, not in a complete from, but as the study allows.

In the last chapter, i.e., sixth, conclusions are derived from the work, from a perspective view, and also the importance and need of further study in this area is being proposed.

Higher education in modern India, regarding moral aims and objectives, rules and regulations, in the educational committees' and commissions' recommendations, and the educational policies are really noteworthy. They are all in 'shoulds' and 'oughts' terminology, but in practice, it is appearing to be a different matter. The important point here is, not only making strees in plannings and policies, but also they must take up the responsibilities of setting up proper measures to see that they are implemented in the educational institutions at all levels. Necessary actions really must be taken against those who deviate from the moral rules and regulations, and are involved immoral activities.

1

Morality and Education

> **The term 'moral' implies conformity with the socially accepted norms of goodness or rightness in conduct or character, sometimes specifically sexual conduct (webster). In this sense morality is relative.**
>
> ***M. S. Gore, Indian Education Structure and Process***

> **Education has always been regarded in India as a source of illumination and power which transforms and ennobles our nature by the progressive and harmonious development of our physical, mental, intellectual and spiritual powers and faculties.**
>
> ***A. S. Altekar, Education in Ancient India***

Morality

Morality or Moral conduct is, practicing customs and habits of a culture. Commonly-participated-in behaviour patterns is known as culture and so moral behaviour is a cultural behaviour. These patterns of behaviour are not inborn, but acquired through learning. These contain ideas, attitudes and practices in which the elders of a society commonly participate. But there exists no permanent code of behaviour in its totality, as the time changes, some of the contents of the code are also changed, or replaced. In practice moral culture is transmitted from individual to individual and generation to generation.

Therefore, it is essential for a child to acquire the moral behaviour patterns from the elders through learning. It is the responsibility of the members of a society to trust in the efficacy of its moral principles and precepts set in the manner of a code to be practiced. Personal and social sustenance, progress, peace and happiness are based in observing such moral codes of behaviour. If not, individual and social life becomes a chaos. For example, the moral precept, 'thou shalt not kill others' if this is not followed, it could be imagined how horrible social life becomes as there would be any security. Moral behaviour is mainly a social behaviour as man is fundamentally a social being. It conditions the individual's behaviour to observe it for social and individual welfare.

It is the responsibility of the elders of a society to mould the moral conduct of its youth through education, as the main vehicle. Informal types of teaching take place by the family and others in the society. But formal education is intended to do it in a more systematic and planned way with set goals, which actually possesses the needed equipment and techniques to form it. To develop the complete man, all the dimensions of him must be taken care of by education and morality is one of the main dimensions, which helps to regulate and lead the other dimensions of man to use them in a good and better way.

Meaning and Nature of Morality

'Moral', the term is etymologically derived from the Latin word 'mores', means customs or habits or character, and it is synonymous with the word 'ethics', which is derived from the Greek word 'ethos' indicating the same meaning.

Morality can be defined as a moral conduct, which desires always to do good as such, Good occupies the centre of morality and a thing is generally said to be good when it serves the purpose for which it is meant and is valuable to attain some end. Though moral is social in nature, there are some actions which are considered moral even when the agent himself is the benefactor of his actions. This gives provision for some self-regarding virtues in the concept of morality.

Classification of Human Actions

Human actions are classified into threefold by the traditional ethical philosophers[1]. Firstly, moral actions or right actions or duties or what we ought to do. Secondly, immoral actions or wrong actions or what we ought not to do and thirdly, non-moral actions or neutral actions are neither moral nor immoral actions. The word 'non-moral' means that which is devoid of moral quality.

But coming to the modern ethical philosopher,[2] human actions are classified into two-fold and they rejected the third type with the argument that, any action could be either good or bad in a given situation and sometimes not immediately or directly connected with right or wrong consequences, but ultimately they turn to be either good or bad.

Human actions are mainly voluntary and habitual and rational beings are basically endowed with the intellectual power to discriminate between right and wrong, therefore rational beings are subject to moral judgements. A rational being is capable of this reflective and discriminative moral quality and he can be defined as one who is rational in his thought and action, who is aware of the moral code and respects it by practicing, he is the one who realizes through reason and experience and fights against it when it has lost its usefulness in the changed socio-economic, politico-religious conditions and against the welfare of humanity. He does not blindly follow the ethical code sanctioned by religious or social authorities.

Moral Sense

Some of the actions of human beings are habitual and the habitual actions are either moral or immoral. But rational actions are resistible and morally expressive and construct moral quality in their actions. The distinction between human and the moral beings, is:

> "in practice at any rate; but still it does seem to be the case that what makes 'people' eligible for consideration, and sometimes for judgement, as moral agents is that they are in a certain sense rational, and not that they constitute a particular biological species, that of humans"[3].

Furthermore a human being is called as a moral being because, rationality in fact seem like capability and skill to be used in constructing a good society.

Moral sense is an inner and outer quality in human beings. Moral sense produces moral actions depending on feelings and sentiments. Rightness or wrongness of an action can be judged based on right conscience. Butler used the term 'conscience' rather than the term 'moral sense'. He used for the intuitive faculty the knowledge of right or wrong as a matter of reason rather than of feelings[4]. Conscience is a branch of feelings of internal perception, and the conscience quickly recognizes the moral qualities of actions. The sensible things we perceive are the sensible qualities of external things existing through the external sense, and the moral qualities of actions exist through the internal moral sense.

> We perceive the sensible qualities of external things through sensations produced by them in the mind: likewise we perceive the moral qualities of actions through moral feelings produced in the mind[5].

Therefore,"conscience is akin to the moral sense, and that it intuitively apprehends the relative moral worth of conflicting impulses which appear simultaneousl"[6]. Conscience is a type of moral feeling, which arises before any judgement of good or bad.

> An action directly produces a feeling of approbation or a feeling of disapprobation in conscience, and this feeling is the ground of the subsequent moral judgement that the action is right or wrong. Thus moral sentiments are prior to moral judgements which are determined by them[7].

The moral sense derived from the affections, is of two types"Natural affection" towards others, like love and "sympathy", and the second is "self affections" directed towards the agent's own welfare, like love-life and ambitions[8]. Thus, the moral sense is a kind of affection which serves in itself as an impulse towards good conduct and keep the balance between the two varieties.

The development of moral sense theory based on feeling by moral philosophers is that"... the judgements are followed by reason. It may be immoral by habitually evil conduct of false religious opinions, but shaftesbury helds that it can never be corrupted by honest philosophical speculation or 'free thinking"[9].

Hutcheson recognised that difference between the 'Material'

and the 'Formal goodness', "the moral sense led particularly to benevolent actions which he regarded as entirely disinterested in motive but as actually or materially always leading to the agent's own true interest"[10]. Some intuitionists maintain that moral sense is related to sensibility and it is the internal feeling of moral sense. But, "the final moral standard was not the intuition of the moral sense; it was rather the actual conscience of the action is society"[11].

> ... in morals we want some principle which will apply generally, not merely to those of cultivated taste: or at least we require to know definitely what it is that constitutes a cultivated taste, in order that it may be developed, as far as possible, in all mankind[12].

Thus, the moral sense developed both in a feeling of oughtness or ought not and a tendency formed in persons taste to make moral qualities. Therefore, moral sense or conscience should develop in human community and it is constituted to construct moral laws or moral code towards human welfare.

Moral Code

The moral sense and moral actions are guided by moral law or moral code. Moral laws or rules of conduct change in different conditions and social life but the universal and eternal moral principles remain unchanged in any condition.

"A moral law is a law that states that something ought to be",[13] but it cannot tell us particular matters and particular actions. The moral law can instruct us in general without particulars or very particular. The very particular principles which we adopt are from the general code. Thus the moral code with its principles are our basis to control our moral consciousness and behaviour.

Moral code changes in its nature and characteristics through social change in various parts of the world. The social change appears in scientific and cultural aspects of the people's life in the social phenomena, therefore, the moral code or laws of ethics also change according to the changing society.

A moral code is formulated, for the purpose of social order and they are formulated through its fundamentals. The moral law is also developed and formulated through the nature of ethical standards and broad principles of the laws of nature.

Moral law is a set of laws, or principles founded and accepted by the community, derived from the human values, for its smooth running and progress.

> on the one hand recourse to principles provides development beyond a code to encased, traditional type of conduct, for codes to be rejected or accepted in the light of such principles, on the other hand these principles provide criteria of relevance for the protest of the individual[14].

In this regard, there is no final and eternal moral code as such in any community. Changing conditions in the community bring changes in the moral code due to their ineffectiveness in the changing situation. But there are some principles or precepts in the code which are fundamental in their nature: "From human virtues only moral laws are derived and the true values are not ethnic in their nature"[15].

Mention must be made of some of such moral laws, to know what we ought to do or what are our moral duties: There are broadly two kinds of laws, "changeable or unchangeable", and "violable or inviolable"[16]. These principles have four different classes of laws, the laws "can be changeable and violable: those that can be changed but cannot be violated: they can be violated but cannot be changed and those that can be neither changed nor violated"[17].

Moral code leads to the moral duties which are:

1. *Respect for life:* You should not commit either murder or suicide. The laws of ethics, "may easily be shown that we could not, without a certain absudity, have a universal suicide or universalstealing, or even universal indifference to the misfortunes of others"[18].

2. *Respect for freedom:* As you have the right to freedom, others also have it and you should not hinder the freedom of others and their development of life and interfere only to help in their development and to recognize the existential reality of others equal to your existence and not to treat them in an inhuman way.

3. *Respect for character:* You should not hinder the moral development of others but help them in that process.

4. *Respect for property:* You should not steal others things.

5. *Respect for truth:* You should not tell lies and make others lose confidence in you but always tell the truth except in exceptional cases where you can save the innocent people from evil men.

6. *Respect for social order:* You should not work against social institutions, but should help them.

7. *Respect for progress:* You should not hinder the progress of humanity but help in its progress.

All these are the fundamental duties expected of the individual members, to respect and follow. "In fact, the moral laws is - act only in such a way as you could will that every one else should act under the same general conditions"[19].

Significance of Moral Values

Discussed above was the definition of morals; the existence and development of moral sense and moral code, and it is necessary in this connection to discuss the human community.

> "Values are derived from human life from environment, from individual, society and culture, and beyond all, from the ideal, rational, transcendent dimension of human existence and experience"[20].

Morals are primarily a part of the quest for goodness or truth. "Man's desire for self-actualisation or self-fulfilment as central"[21]. All motivations lead to human needs and values. Thus moral values are needed for practical application to life through right actions or living at the level of higher values.

> We naturally want to know the truth about things, and ethics aims at finding out the truth about something that is both interesting and important the rightness and wrongness of human conduct[22].

The lives and actions of men who are noted their goodness are probably effective influences in training good conduct. The need of values and virtues are perceived through the changes of the human environment. The changes of the growing human environment in various dimensions, need the moral values and coordinate the moral actions and integrate the human needs to keep in the path of virtue.

The need of moral knowledge if taken into consideration:

> It may do so by way of causistry : the student of ethics is more likely to be right in his application of moral rules to a particular case than the man who has an equal knowledge of circumstances of the case but no knowledge of ethics. He is likely, among other things, to be less biased and more comprehensive in his outlook[23] .

Generally, the higher values give direction to particular cases, and the attaining broader outlook. "These are qualities of outstanding and permanent value in the good men, and there is every reason to think that a student of ethics has more chance to attain them than the ordinary man"[24].

Possibly moral values are needed to the society for the eradication of slavery and social deprivation and it has resulted with the possibility to produce goodness and character.

Knowledge of morality and practice of it helps mankind in its outlook towards life and the world around. The moral values coordinate:

> the unity pattern of values of mankind from the invariant supremacy of the higher-dimension intrinsic and transcendent values in the historical evolutionary picture, in its growth from the tribe, community and nation to the emerging world society- a normative unity that provides the moral and spiritual foundations of the contemporary world system[25].

Moral values differentiate man from the other living beings, directing human beings on the right path.

> For instance, sexual morals are the result of divergent beliefs about the consequences, social or psychological, of various sorts of sexual behaviour- beliefs incidentally which, in many cases, are very far from being able to claim the dignity of knowledge[26].

Morals give guidance to life inspite of controversy with physical and social needs and serve to remove internal tensions. "Man's moraldestiny thus hangs in the balance"[27]. Of inter-personal and social tensions, society now stand at a crisis in several problems in various fields of economic, political, commercial and sociological, etc.

> Men living in, say a prosperous commercial society in conditions of settled peace may not greately esteem, because they will not encounter the need for, those tracts and qualities of character that are most highly valued by say, horse-breeding nomads, or jungle-dwellers, or sea-going brigands[28].

Morality is needed to rectify these evils, which indeed desire to serve the society through the light of consciousness and provide necessary training in human character and conduct. The need of moral values, in their existence should be considered necessary conditions for a more fruitful and responsible moral life.

Meaning and Nature of Education

Etymologically, the word 'education' is derived from the Latin words, 'educare' and educere' which means 'to bring up' and 'to bring forth' respectively. Education also is defined as:

> To educate "is to lead out or bring out", and that which is to brought out and developed can only be capacities that man has but that remain more or less dormant or embryonic until something acts him that awakens, nourishes, and exercises them[29].

Education in its process can be taken as shaping and moulding activity, i. e., shaping into the standard form of social activity[30]. The term 'education' as a formal type is defined by Toynbee as, "by the organised and self-conscience kind of instruction"[31].

Education is an action or process of learning or of being trained, the part of such process, the knowledge and improvement result in that process, it deals formally with the teaching and learning in schools. The term education may be interpreted to connote the process through which experience or information is gathered or it may be used in pointing out the results of the training or the product of the 'learning process'. Thus the term education implies experience, understanding and adjustment on the part of the learner as he functions towards *'growth'* and *'development'*.

Education is particularly a human activity, influencing

physical, mental, emotional, social, moral and spiritual development. It is an alround development of the child. It should receive the knowledge of its cultural heritage from his elders.

The methods of education are concerned with the formal type of instruction. Only the informal type of education was used in the ancient societies. This type of instruction is used to transmit knowledge of the cultural heritage and tradition of the community. "Thus a critical knowledge of tradition is useful for authenticity and development and of these for the first spiritual and for the second cultural tradition are helpful"[32].

The formal type of education is administered in the modern educational system. It refers to a "systematic instruction or schooling or training given to the young boys or even to adults in preparation for the work of life"[33]. In this process education means to train young pupils with rules or principles through teaching.

Aims and Objectives of Education

The fundamental aim of education is to help the individual developed into a real human being. Sir Percy Nunn describes that the main objective of education is:

> We must hold that a scheme of education is ultimately to be valued by its success in fostering the highest degree of individual excellence of which those submitted to it are capable[34].

This is seen in the traditional Indian educational aim of "self-realization", Aristotle describes that every individual has two tendencies, passionate and brutal, the other intellectual and human and the education should help in controlling the lower nature with higher values of life to develop into a moral being. In traditional Indian education, development of character and moral aspect of education were the dominating aims. According to Whitehead:

> In order to achieve the maximum self-development in each individual, education should be aimed at producing men who possess both culture and expert knowledge in some special direction[35].

Thus the education in ancient India, had given importance

to self-development and character development. Character formation is the true end of education, according to Perry:

> In the broader sense, education will include not only what we learn through instruction, but all that we learn through personal experience-the formation of character through the education of life[36].

The formation of character is the whole of the person's tendencies in both physical and mental activities. According to Socrates, life and its value was the free play of a magnificient mind, the fulfilment in thought, feeling and practice of a great intellect and a great heart[37]. Students have to follow the virtuous path of discipline and character as it grants right will and provokes right thoughts.

Education is considered as the process of formation of person's mental habits and their outlook on the world as a whole. Education, therefore develops the person's relationship between the whole human society and the environment. Education aims at the "alround development of personality" which implies the self "realization", "good behaviour", and 'good character'. According to Titus and Keeton, the main objective of education is:

> to secure a more worth-while life, in the first instance for those who receive it, in the second for others effected by these, and a more worth-while life is one that is richer in values[38].

Swami Vivekananda stresses the development of character as the fundamental aim of education, in his words:

> The character of any man is but the aggregate of his tendencies, the sum total of the bent of his mind. As pleasure and pain pass before his soul, they leave on it different pictures and the result of these combined impressions is what is called a man's character[39].

From the point of view of the individual, education is the characteristic of personal growth, and from the point of view of the society, the need and function of education is to "preserve", "transmit" and "renew culture".

The committees and commissions on higher education, stress moral development as an important aim of education at all levels. The University Education Commission headed by Radhakrishnan

(1948-49) recommended, inculcating moral values to the students as a necessary part of education. Report of the Commission on Religious and Moral Education (1959) emphasized the importance of moral education and conduct of man towards man to be developed through moral values. He stated that, good manners are the main part of them, which remove harshness in words and roughness in behaviour. And there is ample scope for the teaching of moral values through physical education and extra-curricular activities need to be more effectively directed towards development of character and discipline. The Kothari Commission (1964-66) recommended the cultivation of social and spiritual values for character building as one of the main tasks of reformation in education. It says that for Universities, their principle object is to deepen man's understanding of the universe and of himself[40].

Education at practice helps the human society to develop. Sir Percy Nunn observes:

> We shall stand throughout on the position that nothing good enters into the human world except in and through the free activities of individual men and women, and that educational practice must be shaped to accord with that truth[41] .

Significance of Education

The aims and objectives and the developmental process of education including meaning and definition of education point out clearly the functions of education. Aims of education should be formulated in order to help individuals to lead a meaningful and worthy life. Education is needed for the individual and this social development.

> ... Education must be seen in relation to the ultimate problem of life- problems that concern the nature and destiny of man both as a member of historically developing society and as a being in the presence of eternity[42].

Education is needed to develop the people's individual qualities and moral conception of an ideal man is required to keep it as a model to work for it through education. Jeffereys stated:

> If education is supremely concerned with the quality of people, it needs the inspiration of some vision of what human beings ought to be some notion of what is a good kind of person, or a bad kind of person[43].

Education is needed by both children as well as adults. The need of training can be to enlarge the scrope of those human thoughts, the characteristics of the natural man, environmental conditions, etc. Education, psychologically and socially, beginning with the preservation of the culture and heritage from generation to generation. The need of education is to bring alround development in the human being.

> Educational efforts must, it would seem, be limited to securing for everyone the conditions under which individuality is most completely developed-that is to enabling him to make his original contribution to the variegated whole of human life as full and as truly characteristic as his nature permits; the form of the contribution bring life to the individual as something which each must, in living and by living, forge out for himself[44].

Education also needed for children to develop a "way of behaviour" in the right manner. The purpose of education was broadly classified into some categories like cultural development as well as moral development. Thus education is for the transmission of higher cultural values and the formation of human life in society. It is needed for the human beings to fulfill the needs and demands in individuals' lives and of preparation for both occupational and ideal roles in their life. In this regard, Kumud Ben Joshi addresses:

> There are two important aspects of education, one is the cultural, which helps individuals grow from within, and the other, the production aspect, which makes the person productive by imparting the skills required as a means to livelihood[45].

She classified the degrees of comparison of narrow and broader senses of the need of education.

> A degree which does not contribute to the enrichment of faculties, leading to find better solutions to the problems of life, can be of little use. In the broader sense, education should enable one to acquire the strength to protect oneself against the many dark forces that surround an individual[46].

People need education for creating the social consciousness and generating a sense of National Unity and Integration. The need of education we have to take into consideration is that it should develop a scientific outlook and productivity. It promotes modernisation of society. It ensures the development of a medium of instruction and National Languages. It also provides educational freedom among the children, teachers and administrators through institutions or organisations. Education trains people's awareness, their power of intelligence and consciousness. A good physical education provided on the physical plane would help the mind to be steady.

Thus the purpose of education in the words of Nunn Percy:

> The purpose of education, one says, is to form character; another, to prepare for complete living; a third, to produce a sound mind in a sound body; and the series of replies of this kind could easily be continued[47].

Education, thus is needed for emotional, physical, mental and moral development to make men perfect consciously, intellectually and morally good citizens of the country. It is also trains them to know the differences of attachment and datachment, fear and fearlessness, strength and consistency in their life style. It creates practicality, integrity of the individuals' consciousness, moral abilities, physical strength and mental or intellectual power.

> Education should be whole, education to develop the head, the hand and the heart, the main progressive of mankind. In addition to offering a key to all knowledge, education should help the child to develop discipline and character and should also help him in his future vocation. Every citizen has a right to such education to enable one to acquire such education, the pattern must be tailored to help the development of an integrated personality with a sound and healthy mind and body[48].

Thus the meaning and purpose of 'morality' and 'Education'. It can be taken into consideration that morality and education are closely connected from the point of view of its meaning, aims and functions of educational institutions.

Human society in any culture cannot undermine the significance of the teaching or inculcation of moral and spiritual values and practices to its younger generation. Those political states which neglected these values in their educational policies and practices reaped their consequences by facing bloody upheavals from the youth of the educational institutions. A glaring illustration is Turkey under Kemal Atatark and Meiji Japan.

Morality and Education

In the formal type, education in its lower levels generally provides in its curriculum and syllabus for the teaching of moral values. The study of morals are essential to mould the student's behaviour and to make him a useful member of society. Education while helping to mould the student's way of outlook takes into consideration the socially accepted and useful norms and values and rejects the unwanted and useless for the welfare of individual and society. Thus the aim of education gives importance to character formation and the study of morals bring out the principles for character development.

Thus, education should inculcate in the minds of the students through the teaching of moral values taken from the religions and preachings of great personalities, regard for the higher values of life. Secular states like India believe and support teaching of the essence of all religions which leads to moral and spiritual development in the students.

From the beginning of human culture, religion has been occupied as one of the fundamental aspects of human life on individual and social levels. To be religious one has to follow a certain code of conduct, based on particular individual and social norms, values and beliefs. Moral values and practices had their origin in a religious background. It became so common to say that to be moral or good is to be religious or vise versa till today.

Thus religion and morals are have a close relation. Joe Park says that many persons believe that religion is the indispensable basis of morality, but need not be totally true and in all cases, and there was no doubt that a certain close relation often exists between them[49]. In cases of atheists and agnosists, they also possess and practice certain moral codes to lead happy social lives. Morals and religion are connected with each other generally and certainly with educational practices.

Morals are concerned with human actions, behaviour and attitudes towards one's self and others in the community. All of these should be utilised by the people, in this regard education is an instrument to communicate the principles and values to the people. Education that maintas these contents in its curriculum and its system in a methodological way is known as moral education.

> ... moral education is that process which helps children to develop their own moral philosophy. And this suggests that they should live self-directive lives based on a coherent value system, which springs from rationality held ethical principles[50].

Education can keep up moral environment of the institution with the help of teaching and practicing moral values and the Morality concerned with conduct, good relationship, readiness, courage, will power, freedom, goodness, beauty, behaviour of the man, justice, virtues and so on. Education should always try to maintain and implement values and to provide children with these values for their alround development, in its true sense. Therefore morality and education are closely connected and they are the two sides of the same coin. These are not only inter-related but also indivisible in the "True education".

In this connection, it should be remembered that moral actions like- doing good for the welfare of others, behave politely, acting lawfully were connected with the training. According to Perry, in the broader sense of education, that includes "not only what we learn through instruction, but all that we learn through the education of life"[51].

Morality is a code of living in the society and education is a social instrument to that end. Morality is concerned with the persons activities and attitudes and education is to sustain the means and enrich the existing social and cultural heritage of the society. Education strengthens the existing moral values in the society.

References

1. J. Sinha, *A Manual of Ethics,* p. 36.
2. G. E. Moore, *Principia Ethica,* p. 23.
3. William Lillie, *An Introduction to Ethics,* p. 124.
4. *Ibid,* p. 124.

5. J. Sinha, *A Manual of Ethics,* p. 177.
6. *Ibid,* p. 296.
7. *Ibid,* p. 60.
8. William Lillie, *An Introduction to Ethics,* p. 121.
9. Shaftesbury, *An Inquiry Concerning Virtue,* Bk. 1, p. III.
10. William Lillie, *An Introduction to Ethics,* p. 122.
11. *Idem.*
12. J. S. Meckenzie, *A Manual of Ethics,* p. 147.
13. *Ibid,* p. 136.
14. Richard Peters, *Authority Responsibility and Education,* p. 145.
15. Prof. K S. Murty, *Ethics, Education, Indian Unity and Culture,* p. 22.
16. J. S. Meckenzie. *A Manual of Ethics,* p. 132.
17. *Idem.*
18. J. S. Meckenzie, *A Manual of Ethics,* p. 155.
19. J. S. Meckenzie, *A Manual of Ethics,* p. 155.
20. R. K. Mukherjee, *The Dimensions of Values - A Unifies Theory,* p. 9.
21. *Ibid,* p. 19.
22. William Lillie, *An Introduction to Ethics,* p. 18.
23. *Ibid,* p. 19.
24. William Lillie, *An Introduction to Ethics,* p.19.
25. R. K. Mukherjee, *The Dimensions of Values—A Unified Theory,* p. 13.
26. G. J. Warnock, *The Object of Morality,* p. 4.
27. A. W. Kay, *Moral Development,* p. 88.
28. G. J. Warnock, *The Object of Morality,* p. 4.
29. Joe Park, *Selected Readings in the Philosophy of Education,* p. 11.
30. John Dewey, *Democracy and Education,* p. 12.
31. Edward D. Myers, *Educational in the Perspective of History, with a concluding chapter by Anold J. Toynbee,* 1963, p. 269.
32. K. S. Murty, *Ethics, Education, Indian Unity and Culture,* p. 3.
33. Arun Bhattacharjee, *Misconduct of Students,* p. 15.
34. Sir Percy Nunn, *Education : Its Data and First Principles,* p. 12.
35. A. N. Whitehead, *Aims of Education and Other Essays,* p. 245.
36. L. R. Perry, *Educational Thinkers Series,* Op. cit., p. 33.

37. H. H. Titus, M. T. Keeton, *The Range of Ethics - Introductory Reading*, p. 404.
38. H. H. Titus, M. T. Keeton, *The Range of Ethics - Introductory Reading*, p. 404.
39. Swami Vivekananda, *Complete Works*, Vol. 1, p. 25.
40. Kothari Commission's Report, p. 358.
41. Sir Percy Nunn, *Op. Cit.*, p. 12.
42. M. V. C. Jeffereys, *The Aims of Education*, p. 3.
43. *Ibid*, p. xiv.
44. Sir Percy Nunn, *Op. cit.*, p. 13.
45. Kumud Ben Joshi, *Treasury of living Words: A Selection from the speeches of a Governor*, p. 34. Address at the National Conference on the Role of Universities in the implementation of the New Education Policy sponsored by the Osmania University in Collaboration with the Association of Indian Universities, on 18th December, 1987.
46. Kumud Ben Joshi, *Op.cit.*, p34.
47. Sir Percy Nun, *Education, Its Data and First Principles*, p. 9.
48. C.P. Khanna, *Panorama of Education: Global Perspective*, p. 32
49. Joe Park, *Selected Readings in the Philosophy of Education*, p. 20.
50. A.W. Kay, *Op. cit.*, 52.
51. L. R. Perry, *Educational Thinkers Series*, p. 33.

2

Education in Traditional India

SECTION-I

Hindu Educational Practices

... The Ancient Indians insisted that while a man is being educated, his regard for morality ought to be developed, his feeling of good will towards human beings ought to be nourished, and his control over his mind ought to be strengthened, so that he can follow the beacon light of his conscience.

A. S. Altaker, *Education in Ancient India*

This chapter deals with the aims, content, methods, etc., of Education in Brahmanical Education from a moral view point. In the formal type of education the general aim is to improve the student's alround development i. e., physical, mental, emotional, moral and spiritual. Character building was one of the main aims of education.

"Education signifies the sum total of processes by means of which a community or social group, whether large or small, transmits its acquired power and aims with a view to securing its own continuous existence and growth[1]". Education has two important purposes to fulfill, they are transmission and transmutation of knowledge. Education is, like a bridge, transmitting acquired knowledge from one person to another, from one generation to the other generation in a society. Education, intentionally gives a certain direction and ideals of a social group.

Education is an important aspect of human life. It comes from the life of their culture and civilization. Education:

> is to awaken the mind of man to a consciousness of worthy (rational or spiritual) ideals and to a lively interest in their progressive realization. It seeks in Plato's language, to turn the eye of the mind towards light, the light which dissipate the darkness of ignorance and prejudice, that breeding ground of all the diverse ills of our life[2].

Development of man brought civilization and along with that, accumilation of vast amounts of knowledge. But it became humanly impossible to any individual in his life time to master the whole of existing knowledge. So knowledge was divided into different branches as many as there are different activities of man depending on his needs, desires and aspirations. Therefore, education was divided into different branches of knowledge to facilitate easy acquisition and specialization.

In the ancient India, "the Aryans entered India by the defiles of the north-west at some unknown date before 1000 B. C[3]". After their settlement in the Indogangetic valley, they organised themselves into small groups and communities. The source of information about the Aryans in India, could be had from the vast literature available in the Vedas. Vedic period marks the beginning of Indian culture. In those days there was no distinction between religious norms and social or moral norms i. e., moral code. "The fundamental principles of social, political, and economic life were welded into a comprehensive theory which is called Religion in Hindu Thought[4]". "Thus it is Religion that gave its laws to the social life and organisation of the ancient Hindus[5]", and the ancient tradition has regulated them in all aspects of life.

Therefore educational aims and moral and religious aims were not separate but combined, as the main aim of education was developing the child into a real human being, who could lead a fruitful and meaningful life.

> Ancient Indian Education is ... to be understood as being ultimately the outcome of the Indian theory of knowledge and a part of the corresponding scheme of life and values. That scheme takes full account of the fact that life includes Death and the two form the whole truth. This gives a particular angle

> of vision, a sense of peispective and proportion in which the material and the moral, the physical and spiritual, the perishable and permanent interests and values of life are clearly defined and strictly differentiated[6].

Thus, the ancient knowledge of the 'Indo-Aryans' is derived from the Samhitas of the Vedas. The collections of verses are called Vedas (Rigveda, Samaveda, Yajurveda and Atharvaveda). Etymologically, the terms 'Veda' is derived from the root 'Vid' which means 'to know', it signifies 'knowledgek', Vedic knowledge does not signify ordinary knowledge such as, knowledge about history or geography, but it is the sacred knowledge about the ultimate reality or God.

Aims of Education

Ancient India was religiously developed much more than other fields like political, economic and social. The whole education was mainly based on religious teachings. In this period literature was the vehicle of religion.

The general aim of Vedic education was, the development of the individual as a whole. As the function of education in this period was individual development, the training given to the pupil was based on the development of their potentialities. Thus, education stressed all-round development of personality of the individual to acquire supreme knowledge to lead a meaningful and useful life.

The spiritual and religious knowledge was not gained only for the sake of knowledge, but it was used as a means of gaining salvation or '*Mukti*'.

> ... Learning in India through the ages had been prized and pursued not for its own sake, if we may so put it, but for the sake and as a part of religion. It was sought as the means of highest end of life, viz., Mukti or Emancipation[7].

Thus the moral aim of education began with the religious aspect of life in this period. The performance of religious activities and attitudes strengthened to lead religious and spiritual life. The chief aims of ancient Indian education were, infusion of a spirit of piety and religiousness; formation of character; development of personality; inculcation of civic and social duties; promotion of us social efficiency and preservation and spread of national culture[8]. The famous American historian, will Durant prophesised thus: "India will teach the tolerance and gentleness of the nature mind, the quite content of the unecquisitive soul, the calm of the understanding spirit and a unifying, pacifying love for all living things[9]".

The moral education was closely linked up with religious education in ancient India. Education, in general was controlled by religion and religious persons and associations. Apart from the individual aim of attaining 'Mukti', the social aim of religious education, especially in the Vedic period was preservation of the sacred books of Vedic knowledge and spread the basic tenents of religion among the people. And the Vedic education basically linked up with the 'sacred lore' and religious practices. In the words of Macdonell:

> Since the birth of the oldest Vedic poetry, we find Indian literature, for a period of more than a thousand years, bearing "an exclusively religious stamp" even those latest productions of the Vedic age which cannot be called directly religious are meant to further religious ends. This is indeed, implied by the term Vedic, for Veda, primarily signifying knowledge (from root Vid, to know), designates 'sacred lore' as a branch of literature[10].

The moral aim of religious education was chiefly related with individual's spiritual achievement. Every individual should follow religious principles and lead a virtuous life. The formation of character is one of the major functions of the moral education. The general aim of moral education is to develop moral culture and create moral environment among the children. In the words of W. H. Kilpatrick:

> ... In a true sense, character and environment are, so to say, mother and father of behaviour, that is character is, indicated, the psycholigical structure which sums up in one organic whole all of the individual's prior experiences, and out of which, in its interaction with the environment, behaviour emerges[11].

The relationship between education and life is applied on the basis of psychological as well as other aspects of life of the people. Thus, instruction should have potentialities to understand the distinction between good and bad, right and wrong, etc. Ancient Indian education had aimed to develop the whole man physical, psychological, intellectual as well as moral and spiritual development of the student. So, the aim of moral education was to develop good manners and good character, these virtues were to lead them from ignorance to knowledge and to the higher ways of life.

The ultimate aim of Brahmanical education in the Vedic period was the attainment of the Absolute (Brahman). Thus, the moral aim is also related with the achievement of Absolute Reality with the achievement of moral freedom. It means, the moral freedom depends on right actions and virtuous life. The Vedic hymns guided the ancient people into the high sense of morality i. e., '*Dharma*'. In this period, student's performance of '*Brahmacharya Vrata*' was considered very essential for the formation of character. In this performance, of character building the fundamental meaning of *Brahmacharya*[12] was to attain Absolute and real knowledge.

Moulding of character was considered as a religious ritual and '*Tapas*' and '*Vrata*' were the main methods of Vedic learning. Education led the student in attaining the highest truth through deep concentration (Tapas).

This culture and ideals in education had been continued for several centuries i.e., between the end of the Rigvedic and pre-Buddhistic period, that was from 1400 B. C. to 600 B. C. This period had high respect on performing religious activities other than duties of a citizen. In the Vedic period austerity and sacrifices had taken an important place in the society. Later, the development of culture, the sacrificial rituals prominently dominated and *Brahmin* priests gained the highest position in the society.

In post-Vedic period, Brahmanas, Aranyakas and Upanishads were well developed and through these sources of knowledge, established the values of education.

Upanishads, etymologically its meaning is sitting near by (upa) devotedly (ni) which literally means to sit down near some one. The implied meaning is sitting down of the pupil near the teacher (Guru) for the purpose of receiving instruction.

> The Upanishads admit and unambiguously that the knowledge of the 'Sat' or the Brahman is neither intellectual nor anti-intellectual. Indeed, it is beyond the group of the senses, 'antindrivam' but it is still buddhigrahyam, seizable by the intellect[13].

The main aim of education in Upanishadic time was development of the personality. It is followed from the Vedic education. Their intellectual life should lead to realization of true knowledge and there by the realization of the absolute. Attainment of *'Moksha'* was the guiding principle of religious education. Moksha means the liberation of soul from world bondage of ignorance.

The students should be trained in religious and moral principles and for their livelihood to serve themselves and the society. The aim of education was, that the pupil should attain the real and absolute knowledge. The pupil who personally attains the perfection was considered to have attained perfect freedom. To attain such a status, students should have 'self-control' and be 'self-active'.

The development of the individuality was based on the attainment of the real and absolute knowledge.

> They attain their real individuality, infinitely beyond their little selves which we now think of so much importance. No individuality will be last, an infinite and eternal individuality will be realised. Pleasure in things will cease. We are finding pleasure in little individuality but how much greater the pleasure will be when this whole universe appears as our own body? The man who has realised this, has attained freedom, has gone beyond the dream and known himself in his real nature[14].

The aim of education from the moral point of view is concerned with the development of the mental aspect of the students, *'Chitta-Vritti-Nirodha'* is the sole aim of Upanishadic education. Chitta (Manas) or mind should control the bodily organs of material desires, thus the Vritti may be the reaction of mind, therefore Chitta should control and detac itself material objects. Self fulfilment through the acquisition of knowledge is the aim of education. The morals implied in education also more concerned with the self realisation and salvation of life and it was connected with the inner and the outer self i.e., the all-round development of human nature.

Content of Education

The subject matter of Vedic education is mainly Vedic literature which includes Samhitas, Brahmanas, and Aranyakas but while considering the Vedic education, it is proper to think of the Vedas mainly. The entire Aryan culture is stored in them. Vedas were traditionally inherited by sons from their fathers as teachers. Thus, the Vedas are contained the whole essence of Aryan culture and knowledge in all aspects of social, religious and moral as well as philosophical directions. There are four Vedas viz., Rigveda, Samaveda, Yajurveda and Atharvaveda. Each of them having its own literature.

The earliest among them is Rigveda consisting of 1017 suktas. It is divided into ten Mandalas and the name of '*Rishi*' and Gods is also given with every sukta. The Vedic idea of 'Rita' is the earliest conception of the moral order maintained by the great and omniscient God Varuna[15]. The Hymns of Rigveda referred to the Hindu Gods and the Gods were worshipped along with the Hymns. Seers or Rishis were the Gurus or teachers of the Vedic period. The general meaning of Rishi is '*Mantradrashta*', i. e., the seer of hymns or the one who has realised the senses of Hymns. The Hymns refer to the highest achievement of human thought and human practice. The Rigvedic Rishis are viz., Viswamitra and Vashishtha, Vamadeva and Bharadwaja, Grissamada and Medhatithi[16].

The second Veda known as 'Samaveda' is a collection of songs. These songs were recited in religious celebrations and in Soma sacrifices. "Soma was really a juice pressed out from a certain plant, which on account of its exhilarating and invigorating action came to be regarded as a divine drink which bestowed everlasting life"[17]. Sama Veda, according to Puranas has thousand branches but at present only three namely, Kauthum, Shanarniya and Jainins, are available. Among the Kauthum branch has more current and reliable knowledge recognised by modern schools. The two parts of Samaveda namely 'Archika' and 'Uttararchika' have 1008 hymns, but many of them are repeated and 1,947 hymns are found in Rigveda also. Most of the hymns of Samaveda can be found in Rigveda also. Samaveda has only 75 hymns of its own.

Yajurveda available in two parts namely, Shukla Yajurveda and Krishna Yajurveda. Shukla Yajurveda is also called Vajasaneyeo Samhita having two branches as Kanva and Madhyandiya. And Krishna Yajurveda has four branches namely Koha Samhita, Kapsthal Samhita, Maitreyee Samhita and Taittiriya Samhita. These branches are have a variety and there are some differences in the hymns, they are compiled separately and are used in the performances of various rituals. The final part of the Yajurveda is 'Ishopanishad' which is related to spiritual meditation instead of performance of the rituals. "The contents of the Yajurveda show how it gave impetus to the development of new subjects of study secular"[18].

Adharvanaveda has Shaunak and Pippalad as two branches. Shaunak is considered famous and reliable. It has 20 chapters and 731 Suktas and Hymns in numbers 6,000 amongst them many are found in Rigveda. The subject matter was Vedas, along with those particular Hymns to worship Vedic Gods or Deities like Varuna, Indra, etc. Vedic people believed that the God Indra, is a God of battles rather than of righteousness, Varuna-essentially a God of peace[19]. The process of God-making is very interesting and the term Veda has expanding always in use with the development of Religion.

Thus, the knowledge of God, worship of him and spiritual way of life according to Vedas is the Summumbonum of human life. The Vedic Hymns, "They are religious songs in praise of one or more Deities and were intended generally to be sung at the time of offering worship to them"[20]. The Vedas are the main content of education in this period. Because, "The Vedas are the earliest available records of Indian literature, and subsequent Indian thought, specially philosophical speculation, is greatly influenced by the Vedas, either positively or negatively"[21].

According to Mookherji:

> Rigvedic education, being purely religious and literary in its character, was for the few who were fit and eager for a

> dedicated life in quest of the highest truths and supreme knowledge. It was thus not meant for the many or the masses. And yet Rigvedic India did not present a onesided development[22].

In the development of ancient Education the later Vedic period in content was related to the practice of good behaviour. The disciple was not only to lead the life of Brahmacharya but also practised the special exercises to keep the purity of character. In the content of education moral and spiritual values were given support to the delegation of duty and made the educational process necessary in fulfilling its ambition and means to the realization of the self. "Yajurveda also supplies the key to an understanding of the later literature of the Brahmanas of which it contains the origins and also of the Upanishads following the Brahmanas"[23].

The literature of Samhitas and Brahmanas was transmitted from one generation to another through the content of education is the traditional India in the name of tradition.

> Hindu tradition places it on the same footing as the other species of Vedic literature-The Mantras and the Brahmanas - regarding them all alike as Sruti or Revelation, i. e., as works not ascribable to human authors[24].

The content of education was mainly based on religious as well as moral values and practices. The discipline among the students was given priority in their daily life. The rules and regulations were maintained both internally and externally.

> By means of these external practices (study, begging) and regulations it was sought to develop in the young pupils those internal conditions (Pratyasanna direct, as opposed to Vadhya), or mental and moral attributes, which would afterwards fit them for being taught the highest knowledge, the knowledge of the Brahman forming the special subject-matter of the Upanishads. Upanishadic instruction or preparatory means to the knowledge of the Brahman, are laid down in the Upanishads as well as in some earlier works[25].

Thus, Upanishadic education laid great emphasis on intellect and character of the students. The general aspiration of the persons to learn, to practice, to attain the aims are implied that,

A Sato-Ma Sad Gamaya
Tamaso-Ma Jyotirgamaya
Mrutyor-Ma Amrutan Gamaya[26].

In *Bruhadaranyakopanishad* it is mentioned that, the general aspiration of the persons, were taught in this period. That means, to lead from untruth (Asatya) to truth (Satya), from darkness to light (Tamas to Jyoti), from Death to immortality, the implied meaning is that what the pupil desires is that of realization of the self and the salvation. This realization was useful, to lead them to the knowledge of the Absolute. They were enlightened by instruction and by practice of the moral life, and they were to lead to the light of wisdom.

Methods of Teaching

Ancient Hindu education had followed and maintained recitation, explanation, meditation and discussion as the teaching methods.

The methods of education in ancient India were the oral transmission of Vedic hymns. The original Rishis, who composed the hymns were spiritual beings who were enlightened with the inner light and eternal knowledge. The highest knowledge was thus built up by these seers by revelation and stored up in the hymns.

The method of Recitation was in use in ancient Hindu education. The Vedic hymns or Mantras were delivered by teacher or Guru or father and the hymns of the Vedas are learnt by heart. This method was useful also to improve the memory of the students. The Acharya used to produce the hymns correctly and the students repeated them. After sometime the students' mistakes were corrected in the oral method. The learning of them was three-fold, that is sound (Dhvani), words (Shabda) and Verses (Chanda) were pronounced and the practice made them perfectly efficient. Therefore the students in this period learned the values of the Vedas by heart, and they learnt it from the sound of their Guru's mouth. "When highest knowledge was thus built up by these seers and revealed and stored up in the hymns there were necessarily evolved the methods by which such knowledge could be acquired, conserved, and transmitted to posterity"[27].

"The methods of education naturally varied with the capacities of pupils"[28]. Based on the ability or capacity of the pupils they were graded into three groups, "Mahaprajna, the Madhyamprajna, the Alpaprajna, possessing high, medium and low ability and approaching for achieving the supreme bliss in their own terms and conditions"[29].

The methods of explanation was used in their teaching along with recitation. The Vedic hymns were explained by the seers. the course of achievement was purely personal and individualistic. A youth aspiring to learn approaches the teacher, who were called 'Vedas' and the students were recognised as 'Devas' that is, those who possessed sound learning.

> When the teacher has pronounced one word, or two, the first pupil repeats the first word; but if there is anything that requires explanation, the pupil says, Sir, and after it has been explained to him (the teacher says) Om, yes Sir[30].

The entire education therefore depended on that tnreefold practices it stressed the students memory power, and concentration and the pupils 'Nididyasana' was regarded as essential. The Vedic hymns were learnt outwardly by remembering and they were realised through Right concentration or Meditation.

> The matter of the Rigveda, its hymns, are the outcome of the first, the method of the pursuit of the highest Truth and of its direct realization on the basis of ascetic austerities and concentrated contemplation called tapas which marks out the Rishi or Seer[31].

The meditation method of teaching-learning led them into 'self-realization' by means of tapas or concentration. The original Rishis or Seers, by their method of 'Tapas' or meditation attained the Truth and lead their students into the right knowledge and 'concentrated concentration'.

In methods of teaching, in addition to the above mentioned, there was 'Discussion' or question and answer method used in their teaching-learning process. The students or 'Shisyas' also used to question their Guru about moral conduct. The Guru used to explain about moral conduct to the students and in the discussion the students receive the knowledge about moral conduct. *Taithiriyo-panishad* contains that which the Guru delivers his lectures and teaches about moral conduct and the necessity of controlling the sense organs.

> Tell the truth. Follow the path of religion, worship your quest, perform the good act, not the bad where our conduct is good follow us; not where it is otherwise. Make gifts with respect[32].

The facts and principles were explained for the students and discussed with them for their clear understanding.

There were three methods used, namely, practical, observation and apprentice method in the methods of teaching in Ancient India, these methods of teaching in Ancient India were practising of Mantras in the ceremonies of different types. In the system of literary learning of Vedic hymns orally, as 'Mantras' in their original form, was in practice and the word 'Mantra' means pronounciation. The students were given exercises on how to recite mantras in a systematic way. The meditation helped preservation of the meanings of the Mantras and development of the sound of utterance of the disciple.

> A good deal of the energy of the students and teachers of this age was devoted to the task of preserving the old Vedic hymns,—which were now regarded as revealed or inspired,—in their precise traditional form. It is however, doubtful whether the students of this age had to face the arduous task of committing to memory the Pada-patha, Jata patha and Ghana-patha, for these devices to preserve the purity of the Vedic texts seem to have been evolved in the next period[33].

The practical teaching method was used and discovered in this age that is Yoga or Tapas was considered as most practical learning. It is also known as self-learning or 'Swadhyaya' of Tapas. Yoga or Tapas was the method of spiritual realization. The original Rishis by their method of Tapas attained the truth and liberation. It was a great path for attaining eternal bliss or 'Brahman' or Absolute knowledge and 'Ananda'. In this method of Yoga students used to acquire knowledge through psychic medium (Buddhi-Urtti). The Rishis or Seers attained ultimate truth and bliss by this method, i. e., Yoga or Tapas.

> The method of this learning is determined by its aims and contents. The method of training the knowledge of the absolute, 'Parabrahma Jnana' is not the method of acquiring a knowledge of realisation of the objective sciences, arts, and

> crafts. It is the method of realization of the highest and ultimate truths called Rita and Satya by inhibition of the senses and the objective, the method of meditation sustained by a life of austerities, tapas or yoga[34].

Thus, "it is a great aid to those who wish to realize the existence of the body, the senses and the mind"[35]. Therefore, the method of teaching-learning was in terms of practical method known as self-centred activity and it involved both mind and body, acquiring moral and spiritual benefits.

The method of observation was also practiced in ancient Indian teaching-learning activity. Observation as a method, the students observed carefully the religious, sacrifices and ceremonies performed by the Gurus. The students also observe the Guru's pronounciation of the hymns of the sacred books. The observation method was concerned with the experience and reasoning for the object learning. And at the same time Gurus had to observe the students for their capacities.

The method of Apprentice also existed in the ancient Indian Education. For the teaching-learning activity, the apprentice method used in this age for the carving of art and scriptures. They used to form and mould the idols of Hindu Gods. The science of medicine, Arts and Sculptures was developed in Ancient India. The Ancient Indian methods of learning aimed at helping the individual to grow in the power of universal qualities which in their development to build a higher type of perfection. This attitude and the methods used for the preservation of Indian culture for future generations through art and culture both material and spiritual.

Thus there was a sharp distinctions which came to be made between spirit and matter. The spiritual thought was highly evolved and the matter was also came to be identified and characterised as powerful movements of Indian thought. In this connection the method of apprentice was introduced. In terms of Medicine developed by Charaka and Susruta provided Medical sciences. There was industrial development in this age. Agricultural instruments were made in this period. For all these purposes, the method of apprentice was used in the family for continuation of their tradition and identification of the castes in their society.

Therefore all the above mentioned methods of teaching-learning in ancient India for the purpose of individualistic attainment and self-control activities were practised to achieve the highest truth and absolute knowledge. Altaker observes:

> In order to understand the method of teaching prevailing in ancient India, it is essential that we should visualise the state of affairs then prevailing. The art of printing was unknown and books were very costly, fragile and rare. The theory that the use of a carefully selected library is the best method of education was, therefore, naturally out of the mental vision of the age. The services of the art of writing were for several centuries not utilised for lightening the burdening the memory. The sacred character of the Vedic literature was partly responsible for this; it was probably feared that the most sacred possession of the race might pass into profane hands, if the Vedas were committed to writing[36].

System of Education

Educational practices were, at home, transmission of knowledge from father to son and to others and later on to small groups; Gurukula system - in forests and Apprentice system, Home, Workshop and field, etc.

At Home:—The most important thought governing the ancient system of education was that the perfection, developing the mind and soul, i. e., all-round development of man. The educational practices were started at home in the beginning of formal education. In the ancient period, education was developed in a particular sect of the people, i. e., mostly educated families, that means, the Rishis or Teachers' families only. After sometime it was developed in other groups of the people. In the Rigvedic educational practices were called as the system of education, first at home it begins, Mookherji pointed:

> Thus every Rishi was a teacher who would start by imparting to his son the texts of knowledge he had personally acquired and such texts would be the special property of his family[37].

This was central to all learning by the influence of parents especially father's in religious, social, personal, educational fields. Thus, "the system of Education adumbrated in the Rigveda thus concerns only the acquisition of the highest knowledge and saving wisdom and not of ordinary secular knowledge or intermediate truths for purposes of worthy life"[38]. These factors are important in the acquisition of many values which relate the individual to the social groups.

In the educational practices in Ancient India, there was the great system of Gurukulas. Generally, the pupils used to come from villages for the acquisition of knowledge as well as all-round development in their personality in the Gurukulas. The contribution of the Gurukulas to train in moral values as well as in moral practices, connoted by the term Brahmacharya. In this system, Rishis were functioning like Gurus for instructions concerned with the literature or texts in their possession.

The Vedic learning process was that the children were sent to 'Gurukulas' or the homes of the 'Acharyas' for education, starting with Upanayana ritual. The word Gurukula is mentioned in the Chandogya Upanishad. Generally, the Gurukulas were established in the forest areas for the natural atmosphere. In this atmosphere the Gurukula system of education was conducted in such a way "that the forest and not the town became the fountain head of Indian civilization"[39].

The Gurukulas were fully free from the other organizations and government control, therefore they could fulfil their educational aims and at the same time they could achieve the goals in their lives. Thus, the Gurukula system was formulated by the individual Rishis. In this regard, the disciples were to stay in the Guru's Ashram, necessarily.

For the attainment of the morals and values, pupils should have self-respect, self-reliance and self-control. In Gurukula life, they were much interested in utilising their moral and spiritual powers for the development of culture. The pupil in Gurukulas was made to help their Guru in his duties mainly concerned with household needs. Therefore:

> that the Gurukula system, requiring the student to pass his studenthood under the teachers roof or under his direct personal supervision, was perferred it better facilitated studies, toned down personal indiosyneracies, and helped the student to

> become more resourceful and selfreliant and better acquainted with the world and its ways[40].

Thus, the ancient Indian system of Education developed social, cultural as well as moral fitness of the people. Vedic school or organisations provided training in character, and skills like military and other professional arts such as Architecture, Agriculture, Medicine, etc. The professional courses generally used the apprenticeship method and was given at home, workshops and other places of work. This system was aimed at, fulfilling the duties of the pupil as a citizen in the society. In this period, "the system of education was fixed and standardized on the basis of certain universally admitted and established practices connoted by the term Brahmacharya"[41].

Ancient Indian Education produced men of behaviour, well-grounded in religions, social lore. In this period, there was certain organisation and machinery for the propagation and preservation of the Vedic knowledge and the method of oral tradition was developed in various institutions, such as 'Sakhas', 'Charanas', 'Parishads', 'Kulas', 'Gotras'. In them was represented the highest level of life marking the high water-mark of the nations progress, from which it gradually filtered down to the lower plans of society[42].

All these assemblies were serving as schools, in this period of learning, in which "specialized in particular texts of the Vedas" and developed learning in various professions to fulfil the social and economic needs of the society at the same time, the ideal of education was to establish the highest value in life of religious, moral and spiritual contributions.

> The secret of the success of these schools in spreading the learning and culture entrusted to their custody lay in the principle of decentralization, the principle akin to that underlying the domestic system of industrial organization as distinguished from the factory system[43].

Therefore professional education made an economically self-dependent the individual. This perod of education thus gave emphasis to all-round development of the individual.

Eligibility of the Student

Apart from the other facts, it has to be dealt with the eligibility of the students for education in the ancient period. In this regard students eligibility for education and duties of the students were important to define the morality in education. Duties of the students in their studentship period were concerned with the same rules and regulations that could refine the students behaviour. Thus, education brought changes in the pupils' behaviour and they should be ready to reflect good conduct in their behaviour.

For that, conduct and regulations were available in the religious aspect of Hindu life in ancient India. In this regard:

> Education during Vedic age was influencing the spiritual and physical life of the individual. The relationship between religious and education may be expressed when we find that education seeking inspiration from religious ideals, values and goals brings about changes in him and behaviour. Religion provided the norms of conduct[44].

For the attainment of conduct and good behaviour of the pupil through education in ancient India, the students should have an eligibility for learning, i. e., caste and moral fitness. It is assential for eligibility and it indicates that non-liberalization of education, i.e., education is restricted to particular groups of the people only. There were three upper classes and the fourth was the lower class in the ancient caste system. "This four-fold division is mentioned in the Purusha Sukta of Rigveda", such as Brahman, Kshatriyas and Vaisyas and the fourth was lower caste, i. e., other than the three upper castes, the fourth class was called Sudras.

Generally, in the system of education, only 'Brahmacharis' were allowed. Every pupil was not allowed by the preceptors, but only the selected ones who had shown an aptitude for study and also capability to learn sacred Vedic hymns. The admission of a pupil was on the grounds of his moral fitness and birth in upper caste, and staying in Gurukulas was compulsory for a student, so that he could live in close association with his teacher. In this connection, Mukherjee pointed out that, "as pure gold is tested by heating, cutting and rubbing, so should deciples be examined with reference to their birth and qualities"[45].

The period of studentship in this ancient period was very rigid and well disciplined as Brahmachari. Brahmacharya was regarded as a line of discipline or an asram. However it is rigid, it is very useful to the pupil, because the rules and regulations framed for the sake of their fulness in education and for all-round development of the pupil.

The student should be qualified with his basic requirements, the disciple must 'inquire' form the teacher obediently and render service unto him. Here we observe that faith in Guru is a very important requirement of a student for initiation. The Vedas stress the need for such complete commitment. Then, the Guru acts as the disciples saviour. Most important qualifications of the student were faith, performing duties, service and 'Submissive inquiry'.

Duties of the Students

Following are the duties of the students who lived in Gurukulas. every student must serve the Guru and it was a necessary duty of the student. Pupils were required to perform 'Sandhya' (Prayer) and 'Agnihotra' Sacrifice, tending the sacrificial fire, Svadhyaya (study of the Vedas) and attending to the lectures of the teacher (Pravachana). Svadhyaya was most important element in ancient Indian Education. Mookherji says:

> The efficacy of Svadhyaya is pointed out by the Satapatha Brahmana which regards it as a form of Sacrifice to the Brahman by which an imperishable word is gained. It is also pointed out that by the study and teaching of the Veda, one becomes calm in mind (Yoktamanah), independent of others, the best physician for himself, with his restraint of the senses uniformity of mental attitude, growth of intelligence, fame, and the power of perfecting the people[46].

All these performances show that ancient education was religiously moulded and the practices and the spirit of reverence for the teacher inculcate character and discipline among the students. Thus, moral and spiritual virtues were stressed to lead virtuous and disciplined life. In this connection, key points that the "Rigid rules were laid down for the conduct of pupils. These included hygienic, moral and religious precepts and the regulation of good manners"[47]. Serving the preceptor is one of the great duties of the pupil. To acquire all the knowledge which is contained in the teacher, pupils should have faith and deep reverence for their teachers. Altaker mentions some o f the rules of student life.

> High morality was to characterise their life; lying, gambling and slandering were out of question. Foppishness was severely condemned. Students were either to shave their heads clean or grow matted hair. They were to take a bath once in the day, but pleasure baths were forbidden. Plain living was to characterise their life; shoes and umbrellas were not to be used, dress was to be simple, and collyrium, ointments and unguents were not to be touched. Food was to be simple; meats, sweet meats, spices etc., were not to be used normally. Of these rules those relating to moral conduct were strictly enforced; modifications were permitted in the case of the rest[48].

Service was important amongst the duties of the students, because the service orientation helps them lead their lives easily after leaving Gurukulas, and doing service to a teacher was also considered as a moral obligation. Students considered their Guru as next to God. The teacher was highly respected in the Vedic age. The pupil should salute the Guru when he meets him in the morning, mentioning his name and the teacher may reply with his blessings, like 'may you live long', etc.

The students should follow the regularities in their period of Brahmacharya, like cultivating the habit of early rising which is very useful in the student's life in avoiding laziness, keeping good health, etc. The student should keep the 'Gurukula' in order, clean and neat and it should be a regular habit of the student. The student should arrange the necessities for the rituals and graze the cows of the Guru. Prayer was also a regular duty of the students, they should pray after their daily bath as it helps them also to keep self-control. Thus the worship of the deities and collecting the sacred fuels, in all their days of the student life. The ancient students were trained in good habits of simple life of honesty, modesty and cleanliness in their daily life. Equal treatment was given to every student irrespective of the status or wealth of their parents. Every student should go out for begging but they should not bed excess of food. They should beg alms only for the good for living, but should not wrongly get into the habit of living for food. They followed moral norms essential for their studentship and life after that, such as 'always speak the truth', 'never ignore duties and self study', 'never leave Dharma'.

'Dharma' is used in the sense of subjective as well as

religious merit of virtues. Dharma refers to the performance of good acts - 'Veracity', 'non-injury', 'non-stealing', 'cleanliness of body and mind', 'self-control' (internal and external) reverence and obedience to parents and elders are enjoined on all human beings by the performance of which they can attain 'Dharma', i. e., Moral Earnestness, and Regard for the spiritual (Dharma Shraddha, Dharma Manahprasadeh)[49]. Such as do not neglect the necessary and useful work, and do not be careless in duties towards Guru. These are the duties of the students in ancient Indian Education. By the religious merit and objective sense, duties are concerned with the morality, "in the discharge of one's duties in the consciousness that duties done only with a pure motive are conducive to morality (Vishuddhana abhiprayena Krtanan Karmanam Dharmasadhanatvat)"[50].

Eligibility of the Teachers

In the Brahmanical educational practices, the Guru should be capable of transmitting the truths and knowledge of Vedas perfectly. In this period the Guru played a crucial role. The Guru should have good practice in Yoga, otherwise he couldn't instruct the pupil in Yoga and other teachings of Vedic knowledge, because the Vedic teaching-learning process was completely based on, oral practices or meditation. Therefore, the Guru should by both physically and mentally perfect and model of a Man himself. "The Guru is not only a model of Man but also he should be a symbol of a moral being" a bonafide Guru must be a spiritual master.

The spiritual master or an ideal Acharya, who should teach by personal example "intellectual brilliance not withstanding a man of dubious personal character, who is attached to selfish gratification and self-interest, cannot control himself and a spiritual master"[51]. Thus, the Acharya should be a perfect being detached from material pleasures, otherwise he could not be a Guru. He was considered as a Saviour of human kind.

Teaching (Adhyapana) in this period was an obligatory and chossen duty of the Brahmin. A. S. Altaker defines:

> The general view that the teaching profession was to preserve jealously guarded by the Brahmanas in ancient India required

> several modifications. It is undoubatedly true that the vast majority of a teachers in ancient India was that of Brahmanas[52].

At that time in India, teachers were men of the highest ideal from the point of view of knowledge and morally and spiritually virtuous life in the society. Generally they maintained their intellectual and spiritual abilities and qualities. Living in their asramas, they always were thinking about the development of spiritual ideals. They paid attention to their students like sons and managed for their needs and helped them. Therefore the responsibility of Gurus was to try to develop the qualities and progress of the students. The teacher who himself was equivalent to 'Absolute' possessing the Absolute knowledge and that person only was authorised to be called Guru. Such a Guru was fully skilled in 'Vedas' and was a devotee of Brahman and also a trained philosopher. The Teaching profession was not restricted to the other castes than Brahmanas, but the teaching of religious and Vedic knowledge was the concern of the Brahmans. In this connection, A. S. Altaker points out :

> In course of time, however, religious and literary education became confined to the Brahmanas, and higher professional education to the various non-Brahman castes and quilds concerned in the matter[53].

Teacher-Student Relationship

The teacher-pupil relationship was ideal and morally good. They developed love without any selfish motives and developed equal-mindedness and cultivated the highest type of love, it led to a moral way of life in the Gurukulas (Ashramas). The Guru-Sishya relationship was that of father and son. First of all, the teacher used to instruct the pupils to control their senses. In this regard, R. K. Mookherji clearly admits:

> The relation between the teacher and the taught were of the happiest kind. The pupil looked upto his preceptor as his father (Prasna, vi, vii). As indicated in the probationary verse beginning with Sahanavavatu which is uttered at the beginning of each days study, the teacher and his pupil were united by a common aim of preserving and propagating the sacred learning and showing its worth in their life and conduct[54].

In this period, Acharya was highly respected and looked at

as a responsible person in the society. The pupils lived with the highest ideal of life. There is divine relationship between teacher and the pupils, and the students enjoyed always to follow their teacher and they had faith in the Guru. In this connection, A. S. Altaker opines, "the relationship between teacher and the pupil were sacred and necessary progress in education was possible only if there was complete harmony, sympathy and whole-hearted communion between the teacher and taught"[55].

Thus, "the student was to hold his teacher in deep reverence"[56]. The student behaviour should be connected with the rules and good manner; the rules should not be violated-if the teacher walks, the student has to walk after him. Students ought to get up and salute their teacher as a mark of respect. There were also rules and regulations, like giving respect to the sons and wives and other relatives of the teacher. To cultivate discipline, they followed these realities in their day to day life, i. e., adherence to veracity, dutifullness, love of scholarship, students service to the teacher, reverence to the parents and teacher and honesty, simple mode of living, courtesy, 'self-discipline' and 'self-sacrifice'.

The teacher, also was under an obligation, with love, to fulfil his duties towards his students. Thus, the teacher should cultivate the highest moral and spiritual qualities and ideals. The teacher, "must have a conviction based upon realisation of the unity on which he is to enlighten his pupils; otherwise it would be like the blind leading the blind"[57].

The rules and regulations and code of conduct for both the students and teachers was laid down and followed by them in the Gurukulas. Students used to gather round a renounced teacher seeking the highest knowledge. The basic objective of the morals in education was, acquiring true knowledge and wisdom, with the help of the Guru. Therefore in the ancient period, the teacher-student relationship was a very important part of the students' life, as well as the teacher's life.

SECTION-II

Buddhist Educational Practices

It speaks very well of these ancient kings that they

> deliberately, and as a matter of policy, proposed for their sons such a course of discipline and education as their best training in manners and morals, and as a powerful democratizing influence, so that by this means they might learn to quell their pride and high-minded.
>
> R. K. Mukarjee, *Ancient Indian Education*

The period of Buddhism (Sixth Century B. C.) in ancient India was contemporary with the Hinduism, and Jainism.

It was started as a revolt against Hinduism but in Hinduism it has its roots. Buddhism contains the life and teachings of the Buddha. Buddhistic religion and philosophy developed from his teachings. "The title of 'Buddha' which means the awakens one"[58], and in accordance with Buddhistic thought and practices their educational values were formulated.

Buddhism is an independent religion and like Jainism, opposed some of the practices of Hinduism. Primarily the founder did not found a religion, but reacted to the practices of Hinduism of his day. He himself sought salvation which influenced others also for their salvation and brought them to his way of enlightenment. His teachings inspired others in leading a moral and spiritual life and made them his disciples.

Buddhism has some common factors similar to Hinduism and Jainism. One of the common characteristics is regarding the intrinsic worth of individual persons, they agreed that the human body is a drag upon the essential self, retarding it in its quest for the truth and freedom (Moksha). These religions teach that the individual can be emancipated and enlightened only through self-discipline. "Buddha took himself at first to severe penance; but, not meeting with success in that direction, he began a fresh course of selfdiscipline characterized by less rigour"[59]. And there is a difference between Brahmanic or Hindu and Buddhist education. In this connection F. E. Keay observed :

> One main difference between the Brahmanic and Buddhist education was that the latter was not based on Vedic study and its teachers were not Brahmans, unless these two had become converted to Buddhism[60].

Buddhist education in this period was mainly based on

Secular subjects and it was open to all castes in the community.

Buddhism was not a sudden investigation of any thought, the Buddhistic outlook was also similar to the other contemporary religions of that age. The founder advocated a practical approach for the requirements of society and he provided ways for a practical approach in his teachings. He criticised only the weakness of Hinduism but not the entire features and characteristics of it. Therefore, "He used one of the greatest figures in the spiritual history of mankind and his life was one of the most inspiring in its lessons to humanity"[61].

Aims of Education

The Fundamental aim of Buddhistic education was salvation or emancipation of individuals from the bondage of sufferings and sorrows of this world. Buddhistic education aimed at every human being that he should isolate himself from the desires and sufferings of this world-for attaining peace, that is 'Nirvana', i. e., 'the spiritual enlightenment'. The Buddhist education emphasises that the individual emancipation is possible through self-discipline. It gave importance to practical moral values. Thus, the main and chief aim of education was attainment of Nirvana or Salvation.

> The curriculum was chiefly spiritual in nature. It was so because the chief aim of education was to attain salvation. So the study of religious books was most important. Suttanta, Vinaya and Dharma were the main subjects prescribed for study. This type of curriculum was meant only for the monks besides these, spinning, weaving, printing of cloth, tailoring, sketching, accountancy, medicine, surgery and coinage were the other subjects of Buddhist education[62].

The main aim of education was to be fulfilled by practicing the rules and regulations of Buddhism. Buddhist education based on the attainment of Nirvana, is another form of Mukti through the path of avoiding the self-indulgence and self-mortification. Thus the Buddhist education aimed that every person should attain the supreme end of life, in support of this and for the needs of society, more educational centres were established which were called viharas or monasteries. Buddhist education gave emphasis to the development of personality through moral teachings. Moral values like sympathy, kindness, love, charity, compassion, co-operation and non-violence are the ethical objectives of the Buddhism. An individual by practice can attain these values. Education stressed the practice of these moral values as a means to achieve the supreme goal in life.

Content of Education

The subject matter of Buddhist education was connected with the moral and spiritual awareness and the occupational skills of the students. The curriculum was planned carefully, endowed with the teachings of Buddha and general studies. It gave stress to character building and all-round development of an individual, to be a useful member in the community and ultimately to attain mukti.

The Buddhist education as its content prescribed the knowledge about moral rules and religious practices. Buddhism acted as a 'vehicle of culture' as it has literary works which were written in Pali. After the death of Buddha,[63] for the development of Buddhism, the first great Council was convened at 'Rajagrha'. The aged Kasyapa presided the Council, an upali, a prominent disciple repeated the rules of discipline of the order. These rules are called the Vinaya Pitaka, the Suttapitaka, and the Abhidhamanapitaka, these are known as the 'Buddhist Bible' - 'Tripitakas, as well as 'Three Baskets of Tradition'. They are sutras or 'utterances of Buddha himself', Vinaya or 'rules of discipline' and 'Abhidamma or philosophic discussion'[64]. The Vinaya Pitaka concerned with the rules of discipline, the second Pitaka, Ananda recited the so called Basket of sermons, and the third Pitaka also recited is the Pitaka of Metaphysics, Psychology and Philosophy.

In Buddhist history these Pitakas are called Baskets of knowledge. Therefore, 'Tripitakas' are the main sources of Buddhist knowledge. All of these, emphasise on morality, "Perfection of knowledge is regarded as impossible without morality, perfect control of passions and prejudices"[65].

Many of the Buddhist works of this period were written in Sanskrit, some of them are in 'Pali originals'. The Sanskrit 'Sabdavidya' contained 'one of the five Vidyas'. In this regard

F. E. Keay mentioned that five Vidyas were dealt as the subject matter of Buddhist education.

> Sabda Vidya, grammer and lexicography; (Sabda means sound end Vidya 'Science'). Silpasthanavidya, Arts; Chikitsavidya, Medicine; Hetuvidya, Logic; and Adhyatmavidya, science of the universal soul or philosophy[66].

Keay observes that according to I-Tsing these five Vidyas were illustrated as follows:

1. "The Siddha-composition for beginners... children learn this book when they are six years old, and finish it in six months".
2. "The sutra is the foundation of all grammatical sciences ... it contains thousand slokas and is the work of Panini ... children begin to learn the sutra when they are eight years old, and can repeat it in eight months time".
3. The book on Dhatu (verbal roots)
4. The book on the three khilas (Ashtadhatu Manda and Unadi).
5. "The Vritti-sutra (Kasika-Vritti). This is a commentary on the foregoing sutra"[67].

I-Tsing's enumeration connecting this following books for the higher course were studied.

1. "The Chirni (the Mahabhasya)".
2. "The Bhatrihari Sastra treats of principles of human life as well as of grammatical science".
3. "The Vakya Discourse - a treatise on the inference supported by the authority of the sacred teaching and on inductive argument".
4. "The Pei-ne which was a work on Philosophy"[68].

And other books like Jataka stories and rules, 'Vinaya' were studied in the relevent literature. All these studies in course of time are for the fulfilment of the highest goal - Nirvana or Salvation. In this connection, most of the Buddhist monks or Bikkus carried further and popularised Buddha's teachings and Dharma Sutras, i. e., three Pitakas. All these teachings and learning in that period had its main motto that Buddhist monks should be purely moral and spiritual beings in the community. Moral and spiritual values can be derived from the scriptures and the holy texts of the Buddhism, vix., 'Sila', 'Siksa' and Dhammapada are the religious scriptures and the holy texts of the Buddhism. All the literature communicates the moral and spiritual values and the way of life of the Buddhist community.

Methods of Teaching

In Buddhist education, teaching methods are important in imparting knowledge. The teaching methods, mainly oral-Dialogues, addressing the message and practical approach were used in Buddhist education. All these methods of teaching gave emphasis on moral and spiritual practices which are value oriented.

The Buddha taught by 'Conversation' and his teaching also contained oral instruction for his disciples, like all great teachers of ancient times. The methods of teaching used in Buddhist education emphasizes that the question and answer is the popular method, but there were also some methods like discussions, debates and lectures, etc. These methods were imparted and connected with logical formation.

These methods were helpful to improve their discussion power and impress the general public because Buddhism was a new religion, and in course of time, it needed the discussions or 'Shastrarth' for publicity in the society. With these methods the monks improved their memory power and logical thinking. By these methods of teaching-learning, the students improve their knowledge on the basis of theory, reason (cause) explanation and examples, evidence, argument and induction. the Buddhist monasteries gave importance to moral instruction adopted by these methods.

> The history of Buddhist Education is essentially aspect of the history of Buddhist monasticism. entrance into monastic life involved from earliest times a regimen of chastity, poverty, and other moral standards and also submission to discipline and learning under the direction of a teacher. Meditation and study were the two essential methods in Buddhist formation. Principles such as those known as the four noble truths, the eight-fold path, and details of the Dharma or law were

> indispensable elements of study. In the early years the sayings, stories and legends of the Buddha were gradually collected together into the cannonical scriptures. Frequent repetition and chanting aided in remembering the words of and about the enlightened founder. Debate and discussion on doctrine also seem to have been important aspect of monastic education[69].

Practical training was given for the development of character and moral values. The Buddhist method of teaching encouraged students develop various skills like writing and other occupational skills. Methods of teaching gave emphasis to refining the conduct of the students. Content of the Buddhist education gave importance to teaching the eight-fold path by the method of practical approach. The practice of the eight-fold path led them into the moral life.

System of Education

The Buddhist educational system was established in their monasteries - residential schools like Gurukulas and the teachers were responsible for providing facilities and training of the students.

Buddhism was developed in the form of 'Sanghas', in India, in the Sixth Century B. C. In this system the educational works were developed in the 'monasteries' and 'Bihars'. These were inter-related religious and educational centres. All the religious and educational institutions or monasteries were not framed by Buddha, they were copied from various sects of Hindu Seers (Sadhua and nuns).

Buddhism was divided into two main sects, as Hinayana and Mahayana. 'Hinayana' or 'Theravada' connotes the 'small way' of salvation that is the way of the elders, and it is clearly belongs to the older tradition. Mahayana the great way of salvation. The Mahayana "teaches that the awakened individual should work without resting, for the spiritual welfare of the world"[70].

In the early stage of the development of 'Buddhism' the monks were living in forests, caves and under trees. Later, the Lord Buddha ordered them to live in monasteries and Viharas.

During this period, for educational purposes, generally the

Viharas or monasteries were used. The system of education was mainly meant for the monks, to instruct and to training them in the values and ideals of Buddhism to make from real followers of Buddha and to attain salvation.

Buddhist education contained a large group of teachers and thousands of monks and they were living easily in the extensive monasteries.

Education was also developed through tours in this period. Monks or Bikkus gave importance to tours and educating people through their practical and real form of the theoretical knowledge and values. Thus, they conducted the conferences for the monks in different sanghas. The conferences were arranged by learned men on every full moon day and first day of the month in the Buddha Sangh, they assembled and put forward their doubts freely to every well-renowned, Buddhist monk. Through the discussion from conferences they would challenge the whole Sangha to prove his purity. The Buddhist education laid great emphasis on the morality in their teachings and practices. The Buddhist education through its system promoted virtues like truth, love, compassion and non-violence. Buddhist educational system gave emphasis on morality with its selfless service.

Thus, the system of education was monastic system. In this system according to Keay:

> Every novice on his admission to the order should place himself under the supervision and guidence of a preceptor, and this state of pupil age was to last for ten years[71].

King Ashoka laid monasteries in propagating Buddhist education in India and outside India also. It shows the monastery system of education was in vogue at that time, Fa-hien notes:

> By the side of the type of Ashoka there has been made a Mahayana monastery, very grand and beautiful, there is also a Hinayana one; the two together containing six or seven hundred monks. The rules of demeansour and the scholastic arrangements in them are worthy of observation. Samans (monks) of the highest virtue from all quarters, and students, inquiries wishing to find out truth and the grounds of it all resort to these monasteries[72].

Eligibility of the Student

In Monasteries, the life of the monk was governed by rules and regulations for their day to day life. The ceremony of initiation into the monastery was simple. "The admission was called the Pabbajja, and after admission the candidate becomes a novice"[16]. At the time of initiation, the student-monk had to take oaths to fulfil the Dharma of the Sangha as follows:

> I take my refuge in the Buddha
> I take my fefuge in the Dhamma
> I take my refuge in the Sangha[73].

It shows the well ordered discipline of the students. The students used to beg alms to meet the daily expenditure of the monastery. The students' 'service' to the teacher was an essential part of thier daily routine life. Students would also go out along with their teacher for obtaining food, taking with him his begging bowl and going from house to house, but they had to return early for the convenience of the teacher. After that the student would get ready for the education.

Thus, the disciple or Bikku had to serve the teacher and keep the Vihara clean and his daily life depended on the orders of the teacher. The daily routine of the monastery enriched moral behaviour of the student. The Bikku or monk could not take any service of the others, and he could not go any where without the permission of the teacher. Thus the disciples used to maintain their life under the disciplinary control of the teacher.

Eligibility of the Teacher

Under the monastic scheme of Buddhist education, the teacher (Upojyaya or Guru) held the central place. It had given much stress on the efficiency and purity of the teachers. The teacher also should be well experienced and necessarily must have moral character. The role of the teacher was to preach Dharma (religion) and train pupils in noble values successfully in the way of democratic and secular attitudes and moral and mental discipline. In the monastery, the teacher was responsible for pupils' health and studies. Thus the Buddhist education emphasised moral character and the teacher played an indispensable parental role in the education of the student monks. The teacher taught his disciples necessarily the Buddha's teachings. Thus the teacher was more responsible for the student-monks. According to Chaube:

> The teacher was responsible for food, clothing and residence and moral and religions education of the student. The student had to serve the teacher with full devotion[74].

Teacher-Student Relationship

The teacher-pupil relationship was based upon divine love. The teacher and the taught were very close and affectionate, pure and disciplinary. The teacher led a very simple life with limited necessities. Thus, the teacher, being a learned man of high quality and character and having self-control taught the same ideals to his disciples and stood as a model to them to follow.

The duties of the students were stable and they were called the 'Sidh Biharak'. the students gained knowledge with love and service to the teacher. The teacher had to protect his students from sufferings and take care of them. In the same way the students also had to obey and serve their teacher. The teacher and the disciples were closely associated in the teaching-learning process and the teacher used to clear the disciples mental tensions through religious and moral conversations. The teacher used to explain the required knowledge using the methods of question- answer, lecture, discussion, etc. He had to explain the students ' doubts and enlighten them with the inner meanings of the subjects.

There was an ideal relationship between the teacher and the taught. They lived together with mutual reverence, confidence and affection. It shows that a democratic aspect of relationship was in vogue. Both of them had to maintain the moral standards in education, because the system of education was mainly based on morality. It shows how there existed a moral atmosphere in the monasteries and their moral and intellectual success was largely based on the mutual relation between the teacher and the students. It was a moral obligation to live in peace and harmony. Keay notes that the relationship between teacher and the pupil was cordial and cites the following from the Tripitaka:

> He inspects his pupil's moral conduct, and warns him of defects and trangressions; whenever he finds his pupil faulty he makes him seek remedies and repent[75].

And the students:

> The pupil rubs the teachers body, folds his clothes, or sometimes sweeps the apartment and the yard. Then having examined water to see whether insects be in it, he gives it to the teacher. Thus, if there be anything to be done, he does all on behalf of his teacher[76].

Thus the relationship of the teacher - taught in Buddhistic education shows that there was great reverence, faith and accession of morality. The Buddhistic education established high moral standards and values among the Bikkus in monasteries through the relationship with their teachers. The Buddhist education gave importance to character building among the monks with the mutual cooperation of teacher and the taught. The system of education stressed moral conduct or Siksha, i. e., 'Sila Bhavana or purifying moral conduct'.

According to its religious and ethical point of view, the teaching and training concerned with the maintenance of values in monasteries such as — self-restraint, temperance, contentment, patience, celibacy-chastity, purity-purification; humility, benevolence, liberality, reverence, gratitude, tolerence, veracity, righteousness, etc. These morals were practiced in monasteries.

These values are practised in education for one's purity of conduct, it depends on one's own righteous exertions. Thus, the moral teachings in education of this period were aimed at the development of individuals and society. Moral values were to avoid evils and bondage and fight against sins like lust and selfishness, and ultimately to gain Nirvana, the Supreme end of human life.

References

1. Paul Monroe, ed, *International Encyclopaedia of Education*, Vol. 28, New Delhi, 1990, p. 398.
2. V. Ros Vihari Das, *Humanism and Education in East and West: An International Round Table Discussion*, Organised by UNESCO, p. 79.

3. F. E. Keay, *Ancient Indian Education : An Inquiry into its Origin, Development and Ideals*, p. 11.

4. C. P. Khanna, *Origin of Civilisation Education in Ancient India*, pp. 1-2.

5. *Idem*

6. C. P. Khanna, *Op. cit.*, p. 3.

7. R. K. Mookerji, *Ancient Indian Education Brahmanical and Buddhist*, 1969, p. xxi.

8. A. S. Altaker, *Education in Ancient India*, 1965, p. 8.

9. *Journal of Indian Education* , March, 1989, quoted Durgavathi Upadhyaya, p. 68 (A Plea for Spiritual and Moral Education).

10. Quoted C. P. Khanna, *Origin of Civilization Education in Ancient India*, 1993, p. 3.

11. L. R. Perry, *Educational Thinkers Series*; Bertrand Russel, A. S. Neill, Omer Lane, W. H. Kilpatrick. Four progressive educators, Collier-Macmillan Ltd., London, 1967, p. 53.

12. Brahmacharya is one of the stages of human life, there are four stages of human life called as Ashrama Dharmas, viz., Brahmacharya (Student life); Grihasta (Family life); Vanaprasta (Life of Retirement) and Sanyasa (Life of Renounciation).

13. C. P. Khanna, *Origin of Civilization Education in Ancient India*, p. 68.

14. Swami Vivekananda, *The Science and Philosophy of Religion*, pp. 183-89.

19. R. K. Mookherji, *Op. cit.*, p. 65.

20. M. Hiriyanna, *Op. cit.*, p. 29.

21. S. Chatterjee and Datta, D, *An Introduction to Indian Philosophy*, Calcutta University Press, 1984, p. 6.

22. R. K. Mookherji, *Op. cit.*, pp. 54-55.

23. R. K. Mookherji, *Op. cit.*, p. 70.

24. M. Hiriyanna, *Op. Cit.*, p. 50.

25. R. K. Mookherji, *Op. cit.*, p. 95.

26. *Bruhadaranyakopanishad* - quoted Vakil, K. S., *Education in India*. p. 9.

27. R. K. Mookherji, *Op. cit.*, p. 25.

28. *Idem.*
29. *Ibid*, p. 26.
30. F. E. Keay, *Op. Cit.*, p. 40.
31. R. K. Mookherji, *Op. cit.*, p. 24.
32. A. S. Altaker, *Education in Ancient India*, 1965, pp. 122-123.
33. A. S. Altaker, *Education in Ancient India*, 1965, pp. 122-123.
34. R. K. Mookherji, *Op. cit.*, p. 34.
35. Chatterjee and Datta, *An Introduction to Indian Philosophy*, p. 291.
36. A. S. Altaker, *Op. cit.*, p. 145.
37. R. K. Mookherji, *Ancient Indian Education*, p. 25.
38. *Ibid.*, p. 34.
39. A. S. Altaker, *Education in Ancient India*, p. 96.
40. A. S. Altaker, *Op. cit.*, p. 95.
41. R. K. Mookherji, *Op. cit.*, p. 66.
42. *Ibid*, p. 85.
43. R. K. Mookherji, *Op. cit.*, p. 85.
44. S. S. Mathur, *A Sociological Approach of Indian Education*, p. 131.
45. R. K. Mukherjee, *Ancient Indian Education*, p. 332.
46. R. K. Mookherji, *Op. cit.*, p. 88.
47. F. E. Keay, *Op. cit.*, p. 32.
48. A. S. Altaker, *Op.cit.*, p. 90.
49. *Manu-Classification of Duties* (Samanya duties) pointed by K. S. Mitra, *The Ethics of Hindus*, p. 10.
50. *Manu-Classification of Duties (Samanya duties) pointed by K. S.*
51. S. D. Goswamy, *Reading in Vedic Literature*, p. 9.
52. A. S. Altaker, *Op. cit.*, p. 58.
53. A. S. Altaker, *Op. cit.*, p. 60.
54. R. K. Mookherji, *Ancient Indian Education, Brahmanical and Buddhist*, 1969, p. 101.
55. A. S. Altaker, *Op. cit.*, p. 23.

56. *Ibid*, p. 77.
57. R. K. Mookherji, *Op. cit.*, p.101.
58. M. Hiriyanna, *Outlines of Indian Philosophy*, p. 133.
59. M. Hiriyanna, *Outlines of Indian Philosophy*, p. 133.
60. F. E. Keay, *Op. cit.*, p. 88.
61. M. Hariyanna, *Op. cit.*, p. 134.
62. S. P. Chaube, *History of Indian Education*, 1988, p. 18.
63. Buddha wrote no books, he taught by conversation and his teachings were oral.
64. M. Hiriyanna, *Op. cit.*, p. 135.
65. S. Chatterjee and D. M. Datta, *An Introduction to Indian Philosophy*, p. 132.
66. F. E. Keay, *Op. cit.*, p. 98.
67. F. E. Keay, *Op. cit.*, p. 98-99.
68. *Ibid*, p. 100.
69. Benton, *Encyclopaedia of Britanica*, Vol. 26, pp. 619-20.
70. M. Hiriyanna, *Outlines of Indian Philosophy*, p. 196-197.
71. F. E. Keay, *Ancient Indian Education*, 1918, p. 93.
72. F. E. Keay, *Op. cit.*, p. 75.
73. *Ibid*, p. 89.
74. *Idem*.
75. I. Takakusu, *A Record of the Buddhist Religion (Takakusu's trans. of I. Tsing's travels)*, p. 120.
76. *Idem*.

3

Education in Medieval India

SECTION—I

Muslim Education

> **The aim of Islam was to develop a particular type of morality and so morality was given an important place in education ... Hazrat Mahammad was of the opinion that man could proper only by dint of good character.**
>
> **B. C. Rai, *Philosophy of Education***

In the history of India, the Mohammedans appeared first in the beginning of the 8th Century A.D. and since then a number of their invasions were taken place. Mahmud of Ghazni, the great military leader, had raided India seventeen times from 1000 to 1026 A. D. and during his raids the Brahman educational centres were destroyed and the heads of those centres were put to death. The arrival of Mohammedans into India led to the dawn of a new era. This period was the rise of Mohammedan rule and fall of Hindu rule, especially in north India.

> **The Mohammedan invasion and the settlement of Muslim rulers in India brought about far-reaching changes in different spheres of Indian life including the domain of education and learning[1].**

Mohammedan invadors with their religious zeal made conversions of Hindus, by persecuasion or compulsion, to Islam. After this, constructed Mosques, and the mosques according to

their culture, were used as a centre of learning for educational purposes. purposes.

After the permanent settlement of Mohammedans in India, they introduced their system of education and the rulers treated education, as a matter of great concern. They brought changes in Indian education mainly in the traditional educational practices. With the arrival of Mohammed Ghori in 1192 A. D., the Mohammedan domination was firmly laid in India. Consequently, the Muslim dynasty, and the Muslim religion was largely established.

In fact, the education of the Muslim period was much inferior to that of the ancient Indian education. Because, most of the Muslim kings who ruled over the country had the motive of propagating Islamic religion. Muslim rulers to a large extent destroyed the ancient Indian education, but they could not achieve success in their aim of ruining the Indian culture and religion. No Muslim ruler except Akbar did laudable contribution to Indian education. India was weak at the time of Muslim invasion, but not in philosophical and spiritual splendour. When compared to Hindu culture, theirs was small and without any magnificence.

Aims of Education

Aims of education in this period were development of moral, intellectual and spiritual aspects of the individuals. That was, to develop an individual in social, religious and cultural dimensions. The main aim of their education was to make cultural changes and the propagation of Islam. It was imparted for the spread of Islamic principles, laws and social conventions. Thus, "the main aim of Islamic education was to make the students devour Muslims"[2] and was to equip the students with all that was absolutely necessary for their moral and mental development[3].

The Muslim education aimed at preparing a person to shoulder responsibilities of life and also to make him a true Muslim, the Islamic faith is infused into the whole life of a person. Education aimed at the emotional attachment of Islam and the achievement of material prosperity. Education is to prepare individuals to have faith in Allah.

> The whole educational system was saturated with religious ideals which influenced the aim, the contents of study, and even the daily life of the pupils.[4]

Muslim education also was aimed at the individual development. The individual should maintain his individuality based on Islamic principles and change the impure environment. The Muslim education makes allowance for the development of body, mind and soul, i.e., the whole being to give purpose to life. The Muslim education was based on the main principles of Quran.

Character formation was one of the main aims of Islamic education. It gave importance on character building because they believed that, the country may not make her best way in the world unless her educational system is not framed according to the virtuous needs of the people and the society.

> The aim of Islam was to develop a particular type of morality and so morality was given an important place in education ... Hazrat Mohammed was of the opinion that man could prosper only by dint of good character[5].

Thus, the Muslim education followed a fundamental tradition that all learning must be religious and concerned with rational, moral and metaphysical philosophy of life. The Islamic rulers viewed the need of reconciliation between the whole work of education and the concept of morality of their society. Their ambition was to cultivate character in their Maktabs and Madrashas through intellectual and moral training.

Islamic education was aimed at the development of skills among the pupil through vocational training. Mohammedans had faith on religious metaphysical ideals and gave importance to material progress also. For them, education, then, is more essentially the cultivation of character than the training of intellect. As Vives puts it :

> He who knows none of the arts but yet has a practical knowledge of virtue, and has formed and ordered his life by its rules, is so far from being blamed that he is deserving of praise. On the other hand he is worthy of ignoring and dishonour who is learned and instructed in human arts but is destitute of virtue[6].

Islamic education aimed at developing man's relation with God through spiritual and moral instruction. The teachings of Islam propagated moral values, like Truth, goodness, peace, love and non-violence.

> The aim of education is the creation of the 'good and righteous man' who worships Allah in the true sense of the term, builds up the structure of his earthly life according to the Shariah (Law) and employs it to subserve his faith[7].

The aims of education were also based on religious feelings and inspirations such as love and effection.

Islamic education aimed:

> ... to encourage international brotherhood irrespective of differences in generations, occupations and social class amongst the persons who are knit together by a common religion and faith[8].

The basic aims of Muslim education were to transmit to the new generation the accumulated knowledge, insights and experiences of learned persons and to extend and expand this heritage, and to develop the character and to make them pure and disciplined. To enable them to promote the collective goodness and to live in a society of universal brotherhood. It requires adequately instructed and sufficiently trained persons who are dedicated to the principles of Islamic view of life and possess character and ideal moral life.

Content of Education

The students in the Maktabs and Madrasas were acquainted with the knowledge in various subjects, relating to Islam. The primary education was mainly in private hands, but the education of royal princes was arranged in the palaces but in Maktabs the children of the common people received instruction.

In the Maktabs the children received knowledge about the stories of the prophets and Muslim 'Fakirs'. They had learnt the Arabic script and the instruction was given in Persian language. The pupil had training in various branches of knowledge according to the Quran. Education, though a hand maid of religion, was both religious and 'secular'[9].

The instruction was imparted and stressed for discipline in both primary and higher learning centres along with the religious and secular subjects. The Madrasa was the centre for higher education and it deserved the name of University. In the Madrasas the students were given knowledge about various branches of arts and sciences, under the guidance of esteemed and trained professors. The teachings of subjects were concerned with the religious ideas of the Islam.

"The curriculum which is put forward as suitable for every boy must evidently be intended for the Madrasa rather than for the primary schools"[10]. Especially in the Islamic schools the Holy Quran was studied as core subject and traditions were included in the curriculum. The courses of study and the subject matter prescribed for various classes in Muktabs were Barani, tells that Tafsir (Quranic exegesis) Hadis (traditions of the prophet) and Fiqh (Muslim jurisprudence) were taught[11]. And in addition to that, according to Nizami (Khaliq Ahmed Nizami) "as Firoz Tughlaq was deeply interested in astronomy, history and medicine, it should be presumed that these subjects too were taught in the school"[12].

Thus the education in medieval India was so much dominated by theological considerations those subjects which were related with religious and secular teachings. Those subjects which enhances economic, social and political well being of the people, were not given much importance. Later there was an arrangement for teaching of the subjects such as Indian History, Philosophy, Sanskrit, language and literature.

The Higher studies (Madrasas) in medieval period and the subject matter followed in the curriculum stresses was laid on religious instruction, i. e., theology taught were "Tafsir (exegesis), Hadis (traditions) and Fiqh (jurisprudence). The non-theological subjects taught were grammar, literature, logic and Muslim scholasticism (Kalam). But these too had a theological Bias"[13]. The Quran was learnt by heart and recited everyday by the students.

Mohammedan education mainly contained with eleven subjects in the curriculum as follows:

> Sarf (Declension and Conjugation), Nahv (grammar and Syntax), Mantiq (Logic), Hikmat (Philosophy), Riazi (Mathematics), Balaght (rehetoric), Fiqh (Jurisprudence), Usul-e-Fiqh (Principles of Jurisprudence); Kalam (Dialectic), Tafsir (Exegesis) and Hadis (traditions)[14].

All the subjects of Islamic education were leading to achieve the fundamental aims of education. The fundamental aim of education was for the complete realization of one's self. The Muslim rulers expected that the realisation can be achieved through education. In this aspect they introduced and provided that religious and secular education through the prescribed text-books containing above mentioned eleven subjects.

According to Muslim historians:

> they first saw the complete realisation of the Islamic concept of society—a society harmonising religious and secular life, recounciling the interests of the rulers with those of the ruled, a society free from all distinctions of race, colour, class and contrary[15].

The curriculum imparted on morals and other socio, economic, and political aspect of knowledge. Akbar introduced some reforms regarding instruction and he laid the principles:

> every boy ought to read books on morals, arithmetic, agriculture, mensuration, geometry, astronomy, physiognomy, household matters, the rules of government, medicine, logic, Tabii (physical science) riyazi (the science that treats of quantity), science and history all of which may be gradually acquired[16].

Thus, the higher learning was comprehensive and profound knowledge of Quran. Quran was the main source of knowledge in all aspects of the human life, which was believed as the highest bliss amongst the Muslim rulers in medieval India.

> The Quran has dealt with the attributes of God definitely and comprehensively but it observes the greatest caution in discussing His Essential Being. The question of the essential nature of God and the world is the most delicate in speculative philosophy. Not only in theology but also in metaphysics, the concept of essence is generally more negative than positive[17].

Methods of Teaching

The method of instruction in the Muslim period was simple and stereotyped. In this period, oral instruction and memorization were methods of teaching. "In higher education, lecture method was followed and there was no scope for discussion and creative thinking"[18]. The students were given instruction through teaching from text books and memorize the verses from Quran and prayers. The method of education was also leading to the purpose of education and the purpose of education was for the development of student's intellectual, social, moral, spiritual aspects.

> We have little information about the method of teaching. Probably the traditional medieval method of teaching through the prescribed books and making students to commit important works to memory was in vogue. It is likely that seminars and mutual discussion among the students were also held[19].

The instruction given to the students for the science subjects required the exercise of intellect and the non-science subjects required the exercise of memorization. Technical and professional training through workshops (Karkanas) was introduced and maintained by the Government. Values in education gained prominence in addition to vocational training for peace and pleasurable life. Therefore, Muslim education had given place to Technical and professional instructions and imparting of morals.

> Instruction in arts and crafts was also imparted at home by skilled artisans and craftsmen to their own children. This training was free from all the artificiality of the classroom. The boys immitated their fathers at work, and the fathers also most gladly and proudly transmitted their skills in handicraft to their sons. But this led to something like the caste system. Certain families specialised in certain crafts, and refused to divulge to others the secret of their profession. Moreover, the boys had practically no freedom in chalking out their freedom[20].

Patronage of Education

> In medieval India also educational institutions were attached to mosques and temples. Whatever was done by the Muslim state regarding education was the personal concern of the

> rulers, though there was a state department concerning education under the Supervision of the Sadr who was the ecclesiastical Minister[21].

Medieval period of education was received a great patronage of the state and the great rulers contributed for educational unique development and reforms. Muslim rulers demolished Hindu temples and established many Muktabs, Madrasas and patronised many scholars. The famous historical record 'Tabaquat-i-Nasiri' was written by Minhaj-us-Siraj in the court of Nasir-ud-Din, expanded education by adopting new methods. The Balban patronised the famous poet Amir Kusro and other poets, philosophers and theologians. Great rulers learned or not patronised the education to uplift the people. Under the Tughlaq dynasty, education was largely developed. Mahammed Bin Tughlaq himself a great scholar and reputed writer. Under Firz Tughlaq, education was patronised well and he established 'Madrsah-i-Firozsahi'. Education really received a great encouragement from the interest and cooperation of the ruler. Firoz Shah Tughlaq patronised great scholars like Zia-Uddin-Barani, Maulana Jalal Uddin Rumi, Quozi Abdul Qadir and Azizuddin Khalid Khan in his court, who wrote on theology, Islamic Jurisprudence, etc.

In 1298, Ala-Uddin-Khilji established the Madrasah, a wonderful building which was double-storeyed. 'Its magnificence' in the words of Barani (historian):

> architectural proportions and pleasant air make it so unique among the great buildings of the world that it would be just justifiable if it claimed superiority over the Khawarnaq built by Sinmar or the place of Kisra[22].

He organised a regular system of public instruction and the teachers were sent out in different parts of his controlled areas for promoting instruction and this produced a large number of capable and efficient scholars.

State patronised education in the Moghal period, was appeared much progressive in religious, secular and political aspects. In the Moghal period, a new chapter was opened in the field of education. Babar considered that expanding education was an object of the Government. "Babar was a fine scholar and a lover of literature and art"[23]. He wrote his autobiography, *'Babar*

Nama' and he provided an inspiration among the scholars in his court. He entrusted the Public Works Department, building of schools and colleges in addition to other duties. All these works show that Babar took much interest in expansion of education. His son, Humayun was, like his father, had given importance to the scholars and associated with them at his court.

During the Akbar's reign, education was patronised and introduced new system and methods of teaching-learning. Akbar was the great emperor and most brilliant of all the Mughal emperors. Akbar had love of learning and respect for the learned but the main drawback was he could not read or write. He was a great man and better than the other Mughal rulers. He built many forts and in his glorious reign he patronised education. The Fort, Agra became a famous seat of learning.

Akbar though patronised the Mohammedan education introduced in their schools, Sanskrit learning along with it "Vyakarana, Vedanta and the commentary of Patanjali to be taught. It was perhaps desired that those Muslim students who took up Sanskrit should also learn these subjects"[24]. It shows Akbar's secular ideas and the thought on religious integration. He was a great religious reformer. Hindu youth took opportunity to receive instruction in Mohammedan schools in the Akbar's reign. "Akbar created a hall called Ibadut Khana where discussions held in his presence"[25]. The religious, philosophical, scientific and historical matters were discussed and various religious representatives participated in these discussions. Therefore in the time of Akbar, education was imparted with a secular outlook.

Akbar's son and successor, Jahangir was so much interested in promoting the education and he reconstructed those Muktabs and Madrasahs. He was himself was a lover of books and paintings. He encouraged the scholars and artists. The successor of Jahangir, Shah Jahan's reign established many fine buildings for the development of education.

The Muslim education was mainly laid on religious foundations and the Quran was the main source of knowledge and the Quran directed the Mohammedans on moral and spiritual path of life. The Mohammedan educational ideals and moral principles refer to various verses in the Holy Quran and the teaching of the Prophet Mohammed. Values in Mohammedan education were - love and affection, universal brotherhood, and faith. Faith on religious principles as well as faith on learning and practical utility in life "Faith is naked, its dress is piety, its adornment is modesty and its fruit is knowledge"[26].

System of Education

According to Safaya:

> Educational system in Medieval India was also not much different from that in ancient India. During this period, education was imparted in Maktabs and Madrasas which were generally run in mosques. As in case of ancient India, the Muslim teachers were also the religious leaders of the community who aimed at inculcating a spirit of piety and righteousness in their pupils[27].

Generally, students were sent to the Maktabs and Madrasas. Mohammedans, like Hindus, started their children's education with a formal religious ceremony called 'Bismillah' as equal to Upanayana of the Brahmanical system and after that was given general course of instruction in primary schools. When the child enters in his fourth year, fourth month and fourth day, the family members and friends used to assemble and make the child wear his best clothes and bring him to the school (Maktab) and admit him to receive knowledge. "Hence students coming from families or communities of different religious faiths were taught in the same school with the same set of curriculum. It produced a far-reaching effect, leading to mutual trust, love and respect among the students"[28].

The children were disciplined under the custodianship of the teachers. They learned Quran in early as well as in higher education, and they received knowledge about Islam and the principles of the religion. Students in this period received knowledge and training in spiritual piety, humility, dignity, tolerance, chastity and trustworthiness in their learning period.

In this period, the problem of indiscipline arose. Hence the system of punishment of the students was started and they imposed different types of punishments. Thus, the rigorous disciplinary action was taken against the students who were violating the framed moral activities of the Maktabs and Madrasas. In this connection, Srivatsava states:

> Corporal punishment especially boxing of the ear was administered to those pupils who were either lazy and did not learn their lessons or to those who committed mischief. Sometimes negligence in doing the day's work, wilful mischief and ill manners were punished[29].

The punishment rules sometimes were laid down and that strokes should be limited up to ten. "Usually, the teacher had a free hand in inflicting punishment on his students in any way he liked"[30]. "And the cruel practice of causing the guilty students stand in different postures was the invention of this medieval period"[31].

Teacher-Student Relationship

The teacher-pupil relationship was intimate and cordial. The promotion of the students was in the hands of the teachers because there was no system of public examinations and the teachers knew their students' abilities. Therefore the assessment of the teacher was final.

> The relation between teacher and taught in Muslim educational pattern also was like that of the old Indian system. It was based on mutual feelings of reverence and love. Such filial relationship was the special feature of Islamic educational system as well[32].

The teachers were interested in developing the children as individual beings and to promote their capacities and abilities. Thus, the students had mutual relationships with their teachers. The teachers, sometimes expected the profound respect and personal service from the students. And the teachers were to improve the students attitudes that were essential for the moral and material improvement. "In relation of teacher to student, the basic principle is the just and equal treatment of all scholars". Personal touch with every student was required by the teachers which helped the students in their development.

Muslim education in Medieval India, failed to impart the

qualities of knowledge without any religiously biased values. The last Mughal Emperor Aurangzeb gave liberal help to Muslim scholars, at the same time he neglected the Hindu scholars. Thus the failing of the Muslim education depends on :

> The system of education in vogue in medieval India lacked resilience and had become much too rigid and non-creative. The modifications made in it from time to time did not go for enough to meet the challenge of the times if it was called upon to face.

SECTION-II

Hindu Education

> Hindu education was character building, development of personality, preservation of ancient culture and inculcation of spirit of social service and performance of religious duties. Special emphasis was laid on discipline and self-dependence.
>
> S. C. Roychoudhary, *Social, Cultural and Economic History of India*

In the Medieval India, the Hindu education had continued in the ancient Indian educational line. Muslim invaders destroyed Hindu temples and Hindu seats of learning and dominated over the country. Muslim invaders could do only material damage but could not destroy Hindu ideals and culture in their essence. Further more the Muslim influence was dominated and confirmed mainly to the cities only.

At that time, the religious and social reformers tried to awaken the masses and wanted to revive the Hindu traditional culture and learning. They tried to preserve their own culture and emancipate the frustrated Hindus. But at the same time they made special efforts to bring both the Hindus and Muslims closer. Social reformers like Kabir, Tulsidas, Guru Nanak, Chaitanya, Tukaram, etc., started Bhakti movement. Thus, the Bhakti movements imparted on spiritual purification and moral reform of both Hindus and Muslims. It shows that both Hindus and Muslims were existed side by side and their systems of education were also existed side by side in medieval India, maintaining their respective identities without much fusion. The

Bhakti movements influenced educational practices and brought religious understanding among the members of the community. It was initiated, devotion and love, based on religious, moral and spiritual values of life.

> The song of love and devotion sung by Kabir is a symphony of the deepest notes of the religious feeling of the common prople of India - Hindus, Muslims and others[33].

The Bhakti movements, of course, later developed into separate religious sects. During this period, education was patronised by some kings and emperors and they themselves were interested in developing it.

Aims of Education

In this period, Hindu education was mainly concentrated on national development with main feature of the religious integration and mutual understanding of the both Hindus and Muslims. The aim of education was obtaining cultural and religious unity as well as national integration. The main aims of Hindu education in medieval India took into consideration, religious and moral aspects.

> Hindu education was character building, development of personality, preservation of ancient culture and inculcation of spirit of social service and performance of religious duties. Special emphasis was laid on discipline and self-dependence[34].

Hindu education adopted the ideas of the great teachers and social reformers of the medieval period. The teachings of social reformers were the main objectives of Hindu education in this age.Thus the cultural and religious unity was one of the aims of Hindu education in medieval period. In this connection:

> According to Kabir each of the contradictory concepts is true in its own way but each is incomplete, expressing only one aspect of the truth. So, he regards the spiritual foundations of Hinduism and Islam as one finds equal inspiration in both, but is revolted by the superstructure of dogma and ritual which both had built on this foundation. He strongly condemns the distinction of caste, colour, and country[35].

It shows the strengthening of the mutual understanding as

well as unification of different peoples of the society. "The great and pure hearts and souls of whom are religious and social reformers were tried to divest religion of its trappings, taking the pure spirit of Hindu Mysticism and that of Islamic Tasvwuf and blending them into a religious movement which would unite the whole of India in love and devotion to one God"[36].

Some sections of the Hindus, did not share the ideas and aspirations of liberal minded, who wanted to bring unity of Hindu, Muslim cultures. Therefore, they maintained educational institutions which aimed at preservation of traditional culture and heritage. The Hindu education could not preserve traditional and educational aims and ideals in their ancient form. The continuous change in the social values, the ethics of hard work and disciplined life was strengthening to succeed simply preserving traditional knowledge through education. The religious, moral and social values in education brought spiritual upliftment as well as prepared them for practical life of the students.

Content of Education

Elementary system of education demanded for instruction of the common people in the *Three R.s.* "The students were taught reading, writing, arthematic and elementary book-keeping in these institutions"[37].

There were no prescribed religious books for instruction. "Such being the case, the education of Hindu children and youngmen was to a great extent free from rigorous control. Hindus naturally, therefore, had a free outlook on life than the Musalmans of the medieval age"[38].

Regarding higher education, the Tols or Colleges were seats of higher learning where the students learnt Sanskrit language and literature and the other subjects as for curriculum.

> The curriculum consisted of kavya (poetry), Vyakarana (grammar), Jyotish (astronomy and astrology), Chhanda (rhetoric), Nurukta (lexicon) and Darshan (philosophy)[39].

The student learnt in those days different subjects such as logic and other special subjects particularly in the Nadia learning centre, "subjects of study were theology, philosophy and politics"[40]. And "in some colleges the Puranas, the Vedas, the philosophy of various school of thought and medicine, astronomy, astrology, chronology, history and geography were taught"[41].

Methods of Teaching

Pathasalas or elementary schools were exercising the reading and writing. "Students were made to write on wooden boards with chalk of liquid sand"[42]. The method of teaching in this period according to Krishnalal Roy:

> The two points of teaching—writing before reading and of running the fingers over grooved or sand paper letters to fix the forms of the letters in the mascular memory - that are advocated now in the modern montessori method were followed in those days. The ideas and methods of teaching of the Hindu primary schools were derived from the Brahmanic schools though these Brahmanic schools were not connected with the ordinary people[43].

In higher education of Hindus in the medieval India, in the methods of teaching generally there was lecture method, debates and discussions were held particularly in subjects like law, grammar and theology. There were many seminaries were held at colleges or tols where famous scholars interpreted and expounded the fundamental thought and practices of Hindu religion and philosophy. Thus, the education imparted on more religious than intellectual and more spiritual than secular. Text-book method was also used in this period.

System of Education

After demolition of Hindu learning centers, the Hindu educational system became decentralized and the changes which were taken place in this period were spectacular and it led to the development of the secular and religious ideals and the regional languages.

"There were now three types of Hindu educational institutions. These were: Pathasalas or elementary schools; Tols or colleges and private schools"[44]. The Pathasalas existed in both villages and towns and were usually held under trees or in the Verandahs attached to the temples.

The higher education, was provided in the Universities, usually these Universities came up at places of pilgrimages, were usually set up at places where eminent scholars resided. In this period, "the prominent seats of higher learning were Benaras, Mathura, Prayaga, Ayodhya, Nadi, Mithila and Srinagar Kashmir"[45].

Teacher-Student Relationship

The education of the students began at the age of fifth year. In this context:

> There was a close personal contact between the teacher and his pupils. The teachers took their work seriously and were as affectionate to their pupils as fathers to their sons. They sometimes provided the students with books[46].

The students highly respected their teachers. Students should humbly touch the teacher's feet and speak respectfully with them after taking their permission.

There existed a corporal punishment against the students who had negligence of duty, bad manners and wilful mischief. The punishments given to the unfair children were detention, expulsion and making them to write a lesson a number of times and inflicting simple punishments like a slap on the face and light strokes, etc. Discipline in these Pathasalas was maintained by the teachers with a stick or rod in hand. It leads to the moulding of students in the right manner and discipline and moreover to build their character. In this period, teachers were highly respected and they were highly learned scholars. "During the reign of Shah Jahan, Mithila became famous for its scholars and poets who were rewarded by the Emperor himself"[47].

The aims of Hindu education, the system of education, the methods of education were not distinct with the Muslim education but there were the slight differences like medium of instruction. There were Arabic and Parasik languages in Muslim education and the regional and Sanskrit languages for Hindu education. And the Muslim education imparted on religious instruction, the Hindu education imparted on intellectual and religious instruction. Regarding moral instruction in both Muslim and

Hindu education, it was given priority, but not as much as in ancient period.

References

1. Krishnalal Ray, *Education in Medieval India*, B. R. Publishing Corporation, Delhi, 1984, p. 11.
2. Jagannath Mohanty, *Democracy and Education in India*, p. 23.
3. Krishnalal Ray, *Education in Medieval India*, p. 30.
4. S. N. Mukherji, *Education in India: Today and Tomorrow*, Acharya Book Depot, Baroda, 1964, p. 4.
5. B. C. Rai, *Philosophy of Education*, Prakasan Kendra, Lucknow, 1986, p. 32.
6. Requoted from J. Welton, *What do mean by Education?* Mc Millan & Co. Ltd., London, 1915, p. 57-58.
7. Mohd. Sharif Khan, *Islamic Education*, Ashish Publishing House, New Delhi, 1986, p. 39.
8. Mohd. Sharif Khan, *Op. cit.*, p. 38.
9. Krishnalal Roy, *Op. cit.*, p. 5.
10. F. E. Keay, *Op. cit.*, p. 126.
11. Srivatsava, Ashirbadilal. *Medieval Indian Culture*, Shivalal Agarwala & Company, Agra, 1971, p. 82.
12. Idem.
13. Srivatsava, Ashirbadilal. *Op. cit.*, p. 83.
14 Ibid, pp. 85-86.
15. S. Abid Hussain, *The National Culture of India*, National Book Trust India, New Delhi, 1978, p. 70.
16. *Ain-i-Akbari*, Vol. 1, p. 289 quoted by Krishnalal Roy, *Op. cit.*, p. 46.
17. Abid Hussain, *The National Culture of India*, p. 67.
18. Jagannath Mohanty, *Democracy and Education in India*, p. 24.
19. Srivatsava, *Op. cit.*, p. 82.
20. Bernier's *Travels in the Mughal Empire*, quoted, Krishnalal Roy, *Op. cit.*, p. 53.
21. Krishnalal Roy, *Education in Medieval India*, p. 5.
22. Srivatsava, *Op. cit.*, p. 81.

23. *Ibid,* p. 83.
24. Srivatsava, *Op. cit.,* p. 84.
25. F. E. Keay, *Op. cit.,* p. 122.
26. Prophet Mohammed, Quoted Mohammed Sharif Khan, *Education, Religion and the Modern Age,* p. 29.
27. R. N. Safaya and B. D. Shaida, *Techniques of Education,* Dhanpat Rai and Sons, 1978, p. 252.
28. Krishnalal Roy, *Education in Medieval India,* p. 31.
29. A. Srivatsava, *The Sultanate of Delhi,* Shivala Agarwala and Company, Agra, p. 528.
30. Krishnalal Roy, *Op. cit.,* p. 33.
31. Idem.
32. B. P. Singh, *Aims of Education in India,* p. 77.
33. S. Abid Hussain, *The National culture of India,* p. 79.
34. S. C. Roychoudhary, *Social, Cultural and Economic History of India (Medieval),* p. 126.
35. S. Abid Hussain, *The National culture of India,* p. 79.
36. *Ibid,*
37. Nurullah, Sayed and J. P. Naik, *A History of Education in India, Bombay,* 1950, p. 12.
38. A. Srivatsava, *Op. cit.,* p. 88.
39. *Idem.*
40. Alexander Harmittar, *A New Account of the East Indies,* Vol.1, p. 127, quoted Krishnalal Roy, *Education in Medieval India,* p. 74.
41. A. Srivatsava, *Op. cit.,* p. 88-89.
42. *Ibid,* p. 91.
43. Krishnalal Roy, *Op. cit.,* p. 65.
44. A. Srivatsava, *Medieval Indian Culture,* p. 88.
45. A. Srivatsava, *Medieval Indian Culture,* p. 89.
46. A. Srivatsava, *Op. cit.,* p. 91.
47. *Ain-i-Akbari,* written by Abdul Fazal, Quoted Krishnalal Roy, *Op. cit.,* p. 70.

4

Education in Modern India

SECTION-I

Education in British India

All education in a way is a moral process but special efforts in the present social climate showing a decline in our values are necessary ... Pupils is development through instruction in schools is to bring them a balanced development of the personality of their mind, body and soul through an ideal life of virtue, purity, goodness, self-control, selfdiscipline, kindness, service, courage and idealism, fulfilment of one's duties and responsibilities, make for developing qualities of good citizenship.

Education Commission, 1964-66, Government of India,
Educational Documents in India

In modern India besides its major religion Hinduism, Islam had established itself in the land as another major religion. Both the Hindu and Muslim rulers had struggled for their political and religious (supremacies). At that time trade and commerce were developed considerably. The Muslim and Hindu educational institutions continued to co-exist with their different cultures. Then, through trade by the British, christian religion entered. At the end of the 15th Century, the Europeans from different countries had started visiting India for the purpose of trade. First of all, "in 1499, a Christian naval power-the Portuguese - with its base in Europe entered the Indian waters, after the arrival of Vasco-da-Gama at Calicut"[1].

Afterwards, the Dutch, French, Spanish, Danes and English people came to India and started their business forming trading companies. They started to spread their culture and religion and entered into political activities also. In this connection, they also entertained and encouraged education and provided educational provisions through their missionaries.

In this regard all Europeans except British could not exist for a long time in India. "The East India company of Britain was established in 1600 A. D. for trade with the east"[2]. Gradually, they succeeded and extended their supremacy throughout India. The East India Company had sovereign power on the mainland of India and they had fought and succeeded in collecting revenue from native centers in Bengal, Bihar, Orissa, etc., which were under the Native Moghal rulers.

Thereafter, they slowly came to assume political power in India. "But the company did not take any interest in education of Indians and adopted a neutral policy"[3]. Their main motto was to extend their empire throughout India. At that time in England, the Government was not responsible for running educational activities and "the same anology was applied to India also"[4]. But the British Government was very sympathetic towards Indian education. From the Eighteenth century, "Seeds for western education were sown during the British rule. Many Universities and Colleges were set up on the Western model"[5].

The East India Company supported educational activities later and the British were more successful in helping to 'revolutionise' the intellectual life of India through the introduction of modern education mainly to spread Christianity. In the early days of 1614, the company had taken steps to influence Indian education through the work of 'Christian Missionaries'. "They had recruited Indians for the propagation of the Gospel among their countrymen and for imparting to these missionaries such education, at the company's expense, as would enable them to carry out effectively the purposes for which they were enlisted"[6]. The British in their policy decisions directly stated their intensions. "In 1659, the Court of Directors explicitly stated that in was their earnest desire by all possible means to spread Christianity among the people of India and allowed missionaries to embark on their ships"[7].

In this way, they were interested in establishing educational institutions in India. But in 1792,[8] Jonathan Duncan, the British resident at Banaras, made a significant contribution to the establishment of a Sanskrit college at Banaras for the study of laws and literature of the Hindus. The Directors of the Company passed the resolution at the instance of Charles Grant who was then one of the Company's Directors:

> that it is the peculiar and bonded of the British Legislature to promote by all just and Prudent means the interest and happiness of the inhabitants of the British dominions in India, and that for these ends such measures ought to be adopted as may gradually tend to their advancement in useful knowledge and to their religious and moral improvement[9].

In the beginning of the 19th century, British Rule was established in India. They appointed a Committee to enquire into the real position of education in India and an enquiry was conducted in the presidencies of Madras, Bombay and Bengal. It is interesting to make a study of the aims, content, methods and the status of teachers and students in the British Rule in India to show how much moral values were given importance in helping a child to develop into a worthy individual in the community.

Aims of Education

Apart from the general type of education, British Rulers started a new type of education in India for individual and social development. They observed that the indigenous education was founded on traditional outlook and a hindrance for development of education. With this opinion the Government introduced English education in native institutions and established many schools and colleges. The Government encouraged the native people to study in their English educational institutions.

The British thought that education would develop the society. They propagated Christianity mainly through the educational institutions. One of the objectives of education was to spread the religious and moral values for the good life of the people. In this context, they encouraged English education and did excellent work for the propagation of Christianity.

> In commencing their operations, missionaries have generally seen the propriety and importance of establishing Schools one reason for them is to educate the minds of the people, so that they may be more capable of understanding and appreciating the facts and evidence, the doctrines and duties of the scriptures. Another reason for them is to increase the influence of the missionaries with the people, by communicating some advantage which they can appreciate, and by showing that Christianity rests on an intelligent perception of its doctrines, and contains reason for the performance of all its duties. And another reason for such an education, is in its procuring menas and opening ways of access to the people, and opportunities of preaching to them[10].

British Rulers encouraged the preservation of valuable Indian culture. They wanted education to preserve that which was valuable in Indian culture and heritage for the social understanding and to replace the unwanted with Western Science and literature. The famous education despatch in 1824, was authored by J. S. Mill. It contained:

> The useful literataure and science of Europe should replace the antiquated love of the traditional Hindu and Mohammedan seminaries, but Hindu media or Mohammadan media, so far as they are found the most effectual, would have been proper to be employed and everything which was useful in Hindu or Mohammadan literature it would have been proper to retain[11].

In this connection, Lord Minto observed on improvement of the oriental learning of this country and his aim was that the preservation of Hindu and Mohammadan culture through the expansion of traditional learning. In his words:

> It is seriously to be lamented that a nation particularly distinguished for its love and successful cultivation of letters in other parts of the empire should have failed to extend its fostering care to the literature of the Hindus, and to aid in opening to the learned in Europe the repositories of that literature[12].

This much of favouratism and encouragement of preservation of the classical culture of ancient India was though to be one of the Company's motives of political standing.

In this context national education in the British period aimed to preserve both the Hindu and Mohammadan cultures "to inculcate a faith in and love for our ancient traditions and culture as against the scant respect which was paid to them in official circles"[13].

Thus, the wake of trading European companies tried to impel the religious motivation for the development of people's morality as well as education implied with other objectives. In this regard, British Rulers aimed at developing character and moral values among the pupils through education. They had always imparted education to produce a higher level of intellectual fitness and they wanted to raise the moral character of the people under their control. They recognised the need of faithful and obedient persons in various services of recruitment of subordinates in the government services. Thus the "British moral values-truthfulness, honesty, justice and a concern for the well-being of the society as a whole-could best be communicated through an English education"[14]. They thought that moral instruction was needed in the deprived and superstitious society.

Education aimed at imparting of knowledge through secular, moral and religious instruction. The National Education Committee in 1882-83 has stressed on moral primer or the prescription of elementary text book for the moral development of the pupil. "If pupils can cram euclid, said Curzon, there is nothing to prevent them from cramming ethics"[15]. National Education in 1913 aimed that, "the resolution put forth certain valuable suggestions pertaining to the character formation of students and hostel life"[16]. The rulers tried to establish a system of education especially with religious, political and administrative motives.

British rulers gave importance to political and administrative aspects more and more. Education was developed on a new pattern imparting vocational and social aspects but less importance was given to morality, when compared to ancient and medieval periods of education.

Education, was imparted for the development of physical and mental aspects of an individual. Physical training was given to the children for developing a sound body, for the sake of a sound mind. The British perceived education for the development of total man, but intellectual development was paid less attention. The National Council of Education in 1906, Juliya Shiksha Parshad perceived:

> Promoting of physical and moral education and providing for denominations religious education out of funds specifically contributed for that purpose and inspiring students with a genuine love for, and real desire to serve their country[17].

British rulers wanted literary and learned persons to work under them. For this, end, education was needed. William Adam thought about Indian education and recommended for its development. In his enthusiatic words:

> Existing native institutions from the highest to the lowest, of all kinds and classes, were the fittest means to be employed for raising and improving the character of the people, that to employ those institutions for such a purpose would be the simplest, the so fast, the most popular, the most economical, and the most effectual plan for giving that stimulus to the native mind which it needs on the subject of education, and for eliciting the exertions of the natives themselves for their improvement, without which all other means must be unavailable[18].

Introducing English education in various educational institutions was aimed at providing subordinate employment. The Woods Despatch desired:

> What we desire is that, where the other qualifications of the candidates for appointments under Government are equal, a person who has received a good education, irrespective of the place and manner in which it may have acquired should be preferred to who has not[19].

From the economic aspect of education they wanted that it should be vocational, i. e., work oriented. With this aim of education to introduce Western knowledge, technology and science for improving industrial and agricultural development of the country. Thus, the aim of education was practical and useful. But J. P. Naik argues that the inner view of British Rulers was their interest in improving Indian education and was not in favour of Indians but in their own selfish motive:

> In the economic field, the British Rulers mainly looked upon India as the supplier of raw materials to British Industry and as the consumer of its finished products. Consequently, the educational system did not aim at rapid industrialisation and the development of technical education, and education was imparted from the commercial view point and, they had taken steps to develop agriculture and agricultural education[20].

The East India Company had the motive of propagation of the Christian principles through education for political benefit. Their object on establishing schools and expanding education was traced with political interest and solidarity. In this situation they established educational centres in main cities, Calcutta, Madras, and Banaras Sanskrit College. Thus, the aim of education in British India was imparting Western culture. Indian education was meant to be the basis to the 'exercise of imperial power'. Mill opines that education was for" ... liberty and representative Government". According to him education was the keystone to the virtues of a popular representative government,[21] Mill wrote on this view point on education:

> The first element of good Government being the virtue and intelligence of the human beings composing the community, the most important point of excellence which any form of Government may posses is to promote the virtue and intelligence of the people themselves[22].

The Director through their Despatches (1827) stressed that "the first object of the improved education should be to prepare a body of individuals for discharging public duties"[23]. They thought that it is possible through implementation of English education in India. Thus the aim of introducing English education in India was:

> We rely chiefly on their being, through a familiarity with European literature and sciences, imbued with the ideas and feelings of civilized Europe, on the general cultivation of their understandings, and specially on the instruction in the principles of morals and general jurisprudence[24].

British rulers aimed that the education should contribute among people, of their "intelligence and morality for higher employment in the civil administration of India"[25]. In this connection the British had support from the Native people. In this regard, "a section of the educated Indians demanded English education and Government needed English educated Indian"[26]. Some Indians were interested in the British system of education.

Content of Education

During the East India Company's rule the Missionaries introduced and encouraged to development of educational programmes in India. Earlier stage of education in teaching the subjects "were not very ambitious and compraised only the three Rs and accounts"[27]. Indians were encouraged in learning, particularly, in writing, for the purpose of writing letters and petitions and the account was to be imparted to develop the students memory power and the company's aim was instructing accounts for the benefit of their company workers. "Teaching in schools was in close touch with the life outside"[28].

British Rulers opened a number of educational institutions for educating pupil in all stages of learning especially, among the higher class families. The development of British education in India:

> Instead of keeping real academic needs in view, the requirements of service were kept in the fore-front and the Universities were considered as mere instruments for conducting examinations for the selection of candidates for Government posts[29].

In this regard, Government made provisions for imparting professional and vocational training. The subjects offered for study; Arithmetic, Geometry, Algebra, History, Geography, Philosophy and Astrology, etc., and for the maintenance of their religious neutrality. Encouraging native people in education was continued with subjects in educational institutions:

> National education, it was said, must live in an atmosphere of proud and glorious patriotism; must up hold, Indian ideals of devotion, wisdom and morality; must be. permeated by the Indian, religious spirit and must be largely devoted to the

> study of Indian literature, Indian history. Indian science in art, politics, was colonialism, manufactures, trade and commerce[30].

Further development of education under British rule was that an Education Commission was appointed in 1882, under the Chairmanship of William Hunter. The Commission aimed to eradicate the defects and improve qualitative and purposeful education. The Commission imparted education from Primary to University level, but it is opined that primary education must be 'lifeoriented' practical and purposeful. In this regard, the Commission 'Visualized' the need and purpose of 'widening' the subjects to instruct the children through introducing practical subjects:

> ...Like native methods of arithmetic, accounts and mensuration, the elements of natural and physical sciences and their application to agriculture, health and the industrial arts. At the same time, the Commission stressed the need for maintaining elasticity by discouraging a uniformity of text books and curricula throughout India[31].

Furthermore, British Rulers contributed the development of moral values in education and aimed to improve the ideology and better feelings among the students. In this respect, the Hunter Commission observed: "The declared neutrality of the state forbids its connecting institutions directly maintained by it with any form of faith"[32]. Thus the Commission observed the absence of Religious education in the school curriculum and the Commission recommended:

> that an attempt be made to prepare a moral textbook based on the fundamental principles of natural religion; and that the principal or one of the Professors in each college should deliver in every session, a series of lectures on the duties of a man and a citizen[33].

The improvements in education, the Calcutta University Commission (1917) or the Sadler Commission[34] recommended that there should be a closer cooperation and relationship between colleges and Universities. The Commission made provisions for improving instructions in various courses in engineering, medicine, law, agriculture and technological courses.

This period of education imparted for students achievement in various branches of knowledge such as arts, science and technology. The Hartog Committee Report (1929)[35] observed that University and collegiate education, as well as primary and secondary education become more scientific. It recommended for the reconstruction of the curriculum:

> Curriculum of the primary schools should be made more liberal and scientific in accordance with the circumstances and environment, and due attention should also be paid to the fact that it is of practical value to the students in life[36].

British rulers developed the subjects in education from primary to University in both practical and vocational areas.

Methods of Teaching

Education given in this period provided a formal type instruction in schools and colleges (Pathasalas or Maktabs). Instruction was provided through theoretical instruction in classroom in one hand, and on the other hand, the instruction was given by practical approach. Practical training was provided for the development of skills and professional experience. Teaching methods were used in this period, on oriental aspects and further, introduced new Western patterns concerned with the development of science and technology.

Lord Curzon contributed to the development of modern instruction in the moral and secular values in education:

> In Government institutions, the instruction is, and must continue to be exclusively secular. In such cases the remedy for the evil tendencies noticed above is to be sought, not so much in any formal methods of teaching conduct by means of moral text-books or primary of personal ethics as in the influence of carefully selected and trained teachers the maintenance of a hostels, the proper selection of text-books, such as biographics, which teach by example, and above all in the association of teachers and pupils in the common interests of their daily life[37].

For the development of education, Britishers introduced the English language, it could be imparted to the young men for practical and developmental purposes. Therefore, English language was taught well and scientifically, using modern methods.

The Hartog Committee Report (1929) was mainly concerned with the higher education. The report contained with the modern methods for instruction and for the great achievements of the Universities and students:

> Many of the Universities and Colleges show marked improvement in their methods of teaching and in the amount of original work which they have produced; and in some of them there is undoubtedly a better training for corporate life than formerly. But the theory that a University exists mainly, if not solely, to pass students through examinations still finds too large acceptance in India, and we wish that there were more signs that the Universities regarded the training of broadminded, tolerant and self-reliant citizens as one of their primary functions. They have been hampered in their work by being overcrowded with students who are not fitted by capacity for University education and of whom many would be far more likely to succeed in other careers[38].

System of Education

The modern educational system in this country was initiated by despatch of 1854. The Despatch was written at the instance of Charles Wood, who was the President of the Board of Control. This document was considered as 'Magna Charta' of English Education in India. "It was the first authoritative declaration on the part of the British Parliament about the educational policy to be followed in India"[39].

To make education fit the needs of the people and the growing needs of the company's administration, the Despatch took the responsibilities of the development of education in India. "It is a scheme, which tried to touch all aspects of Indian education, right from the primary to the University stage"[40]. The Despatch observed that:

> Among many subjects of importance none can have a stronger claim to our attention than that of education. It is one of our most sacred duties, to be the means, as far as it lies, of conferring up on the natives of India those vast moral and material blessings which flow from the general diffusion of useful knowledge, and which India may, under providence, derive from her connexion with England[41].

Thus, the system of education faced revolutionary changes and expanded the subjects in curriculum and spread over the English Education. The Despatch "partially recognised the value of Indian culture, and at the same time it showed the need for gratifying European knowledge on it"[42]. The system of education imparted on the improvement of the individuals as well as for the society in various aspects of knowledge and skills. Macaulay (1835), who was a policy maker, felt:

> We must at present do our best to form a class who may be interpreters between us and the millions whom we govern, a class of persons Indian in blood and colour, but English in tastes, in opinions, in morals, and intellect. To the class we may leave it to refine the vernacular dialectics of the country, to enrich those dialects with terms of science borrowed from the Western nomenclature, and render them by degree fir vehicles for knowledge to the great mass of the population[43].

The system of education insisted mainly 'anglicising' of learning. "The ethical concern for the improvement of the minds and morals of the Indian subjects under scored the zeal for Anglicising"[44]. Education provided through missionaries encouraged native education. The English system of education, policy statements given to the Government and private institutions regarding the pursuance of religious, moral and spiritual instruction.

The Hunter Commission (1882) made an investigation regarding the whole system of education and the Commission suggested imparting returns to education:

> We therefore, recommend that in upper classes of high schools there by two divisions; one leading to the entrance examination of the Universities, the other of a more practical character, intended to fit youths for commercial or non-literary pursuits[45].

Apart from higher education, as a result of great expansion of secondary education, most of the students passed the matriculation and joined the colleges for further education because the Government needed and offered to take in various services in Public Offices for the University degree holders. In this regard, the colleges and Universities were established. In this respect, higher education was encouraged and Universities imparted both Western and Indian knowledge:

> most of the colleges and schools teaching was essential and contained within which the alphabet was taught under the same roof with classes reading Shakespeare, the Calculus, Smith's wealth of Nations, and the Ramayana[46].

In the development of education, the educational policy and the system of education took further steps for all the stages of education. Lord Curzon encouraged and also developed education, his contribution "to India was the creation of the Department of Archaeology"[47]. In this conception, he encouraged the preservation of Indian culture and heritage through the creation of department of archaeology. He considered that continuing the moral and secular values in education was importent.

With all the aims and objectives of British education in India systematised the education in their nation's model, they offered many subjects teaching in all stages of education. "But there is a basic truth in the view that English education in India failed to fulfil the moralistic beliefs behind it"[48]. The British education in India developed a new outlook on the social and political awareness of the Indian people through the initiation of the British model in Indian education. They developed the humanistic beliefs and faith of the native people. The British moral concern was essentially for developing a social ethos, it evidently shows their democratic vision.

In 1885, the Indian National Congress was established. The feeling of nationalism and patriotism was created by the Indian National Congress. At that time, most of the educated Indians were influenced by the ideals of freedom, independence, sacrifice and national morality by the Great Indians like Swami Dayananda Saraswati, Rajaram Mohan Roy, G. B. Tilak, Ayangar and many others undertook the National service. At that moment, the pattern of education in India had a lot of changes. J. A. R. Merriott wrote:

> For the improvement of education as for the elevation of mankind, the - Victorian had a simple receipt: Imitate England.

> Imitate English political institutions, imitate English sport, learn the English language, study English literature, English history and English Philosophy. This robust faith in all things English was magnificent; but it was not science nor even, perhaps politics. It paid too little need to differences of tradition and of race, and to the stage of civilisation which the recipients of such unquestionable benefits had reached[49].

But, the modern Indian educators like Swami Dayananda Saraswati and others gave stress to the ancient ideals of education in India. Thus the great Indian educators like Vivekananda, Rajaram Mohan Roy and others took up their works and tried to develop their ideals of life in all parts of the country through their established societies like Arya samaj, Brahma Samaj and Ramakrishna Mission and so on.

Swami Vivekananda established Rama Krishna Mission for the service to and development of Indians through propagation of higher ideals and of training and transmitting moral and spiritual values for the building up of people's good character.

In 1898, Benaras Hindu University was founded by Pandit Madan Mohan Malaviya on the basis of ancient and Hindu ideals. British Rulers gave an emphasis to the development of education in India, and introduced many educational reforms and commissions.

The Indian University Commission (1904), once again re-organised the policy of chartered act of 1854 concerned with religious instruction:

> The British moral concern was essentially one for developing a social ethos, and while it is true that the standards of one society cannot be validity applied to another, nor can moral issues be separated from the decisions factor of economics[50].

And the British era of Indian education emphasised that the development of practical, technical progress in instruction, "the moral notions derived from English education have led to a withering distrusts of the national character"[51].

Teachers-students Relationship

Generally, teachers were 'Brahmins' who were working in

teaching profession, but some Morathas, Bhandanees, Kumbis, Warns, etc., were also working as teachers. "The Pandits were mostly Brahmins"[52]. For the improvement of standards in teaching, the British rulers stressed training of teachers. The Hunter Commission recommended that there should be adequate inspection and proper training of teachers for improving the standards. The Commission suggested that there was the need for proper organisation and conducting the examinations and practice of training for teachers[53].

The School teachers were always remembered in the hearts of the students and respected by them. The teachers received substantial presents from the students. School masters were invited to all festivals and great dinners, indicates the respect of the teacher in the society:

> The teachers who taught in the common elementary schools of the time were required to teach the rudiments of the three R's knowledge of the multiplication and other tables in their long and complicated array was essential to every teacher, but beyond that a tolerably good handwriting and ability to read simple writing formed the minimum attainments of a common school master[54].

For the development of primary education Curzon has contributed with his educational reforms. Curzon emphasised the importance of training of primary teachers, Ravision of Curricula for the development of Indian intellect and the capacity for reasoning. The resolution of 1904, reiterated the policy of control, 'Unity' and 'efficiency' for future educational development[55].

The teacher-pupil relationship, was mostly concerned with the teaching-learning in schools and colleges. There was no comparision with the ancient period for the teacher-student relationship in the British period. The Teacher-pupil relationship was considerably changed in education in British India.

SECTION-II

Education in Post-Independence India

The cultivation of moral, social and spiritual values should be emphasised. Curricular and co-curricular programmes should include the study of humanism based on mutual appreciation of international cultured values and the growing solidarity of mankind.

Report of the Committee of the Members of Parliament on National Policy of Education of Government of India (1967)

India has won its freedom from the foreign rulers, after a long struggle. Educational institutions in post-Independence India had to be reestablished to meet the needs and aspirations of new India.

The aim of Post-Independence Indian Education is "the creation of healthy, moral, useful citizens for our society".[56] Before Independence, these elements of educational ideals were neglected because, the British rulers mainly concentrated on political and administrative aspect of development in education. In the Post-Independence period, the great Indian leaders and national reformers wanted to attain the higher values of education as in ancient period. In the Post-Independence period, political, economical, and social changes had occurred, which in their turn, brought educational changes.

The changes in the educational field, after Independence, were mainly influenced by the Western models. The politics of education as a :

> Branch of educational studies concerned with the Government of an educational system or institution and with the political thought influencing its growth and development concerned with authority in education in all its forms with reference to educational purposes, functions and operations[57].

Before Independence itself, India lost its financial balance with the British, which led to the post-war collapse in Indian industry and other commercial centres. Thus the Indian Government thought that to reconstruct the Indian economic conditions and to improve the productivity in all fields of the country, especially in agricultural and industrial fields. For this purpose, education in this period supported the technical, agricultural and craft-centered instruction.

Thus the social situation was also completely changed after Independence. The society was free from the evils of slavery and isolation. Post-Independence Indian education hoped that education should be established in coordination and integration with the democratic ideals of the country.

Education was planned to lead the people on the path of cultural, democratic, and moral development of life and for this, individual development is essential. In modern India, education is also aimed at the development of Scientific and Technological knowledge. Science has occupied a high place in Indian educational system.

> It is to guide man in the evolving dynamism through which he shapes himself as a human person armed with knowledge, strength of judgement, and moral virtues—while at the same time conveying to him the spiritual heritage of the nation and the civilization in which he is involved, and preserving in this way the century-old achievements of generations[58].

The cultural transmission was made essential in the educational programme as an important function of it, which would be useful for the development of intelligence and the vitality of individuals. Along with the development of the spiritual and moral aspects and the preservation of the cultural heritage of India, youth education was planned to provide job opportunities by imparting to them knowledge and skills in specific fields. All-round development of an individual was planned in education. In this connection, physical, emotional, mental, moral and spiritual development of a student is taken into consideration.

Education for character building is an essential aim. Ancient Indian thinkers laid stress on character training and they considered character more important than intellect. It was also an important aim of post-Independence Indian education, and here one can perceive the revivalism in education, that the ancient values were taken into consideration in post-Independence period of education, but his revivalism is limited to the recommendations of the various educational commissions. Sometimes it appeared that, the development of Indian education was a reversal of the revival.

Moral education as one of the aims of education was introduced in the curriculum, "that moral education should be regarded as the chief aim of education"[59]. Moral education chiefly aimed at building character. Character building is possible through education. Gandhi says "any science which does not help to build character is no science at all"[60]. Thus the character building is possible through the harmonious development of the individual. "All knowledge is useless without a good character"[61]. Moral education should be for the whole life, the study of ethics is essential for discovering the principles of moral life. Thus moral education aimed for the realisation of the ultimate good. Therefore, moral education is not only theoretical, but also it is pragmatic. Moral practices like telling truth, respect for others, sympathy, helping the needy, etc., should be inculcated in the behaviour of the youth.

The system of education in this period had developed different branches of knowledge at all levels of education. Primary, secondary, and higher levels of education are interrelated with each other.

> The various stages of education are however, so closely interlinked that it is not possible to lay down any strict order or priorities amongst them, so far, at any rate, as the improvement of the existing facilities in concerned, better primary or basic education depends on better teachers, who can only be supplied if standards of secondary education are generally improved, and this, in turn, depends on the provision of better teachers, who are educated in the Universities and are prepared for their profession in the training colleges, that is why, it is necessary to ensure that there is a general advance and improvement on all fronts[62].

Morality and Education at Primary Level

In 1956, the Government of India, to observe the primary stage of education appointed 'Assessment Committee' on Basic education. The Compulsory Universal Basic Education was recommended in the schools. Primary education is developed through the District Boards, Local Boards and Municipalities. The Medium of instruction is mother-tongue for primary education and the most important development in the field of education had been acceptance of basic education in some parts of the country as the pattern for the education of age group 6-14 years of the children. Primary Basic education is based on some useful handicraft from both its educational and productive aspects. The primary stage education is remodeled mainly on the basis of basic education.

The Assessment Committee observed the primary education at various levels. The Committee recommended the establishment of primary or basic schools, and to provide training for teachers and the organisers. The Committee supported Gandhian thought on basic education, i. e., the craft-centred education for the development of skills and abilities as well as values of social awareness and responsibility.

> Promotion of a moral and spiritual outlook through the understanding of the fundamental unity of men, irrespective of caste, creed and colur. At all levels of education, suitable plans of action should be evolved to realise these values. The teachers and students should be involved in the formulation, organisation and implementation of these programmes[63].

Moral Studies as Part and Parcel of Curriculum

Moral instruction at the primary stage was made important, in fact, moral education, should begin from the earliest childhood. Home is considered the first influencing place for the child. Habits, both of body and mind, form in the childrens at an early age and persist to influence them throughout their life.

Children observe everything and learn with experiences, primarily they learn perceptual knowledge. Thus, they generally imitate their elders, i. e., mainly, parents and teachers. Parents or teachers "should endeavour to place beore the children for imitation all that is good, and should avoid placing before him anything that is bad"[64]. Thus, education helps them to bring up and mould their behaviour in a better way. "The child's mind is every moment receiving occasion of new words followed by new ideas, word, thought and action often come in the order in which they are just stated"[65].

In India, after Independence, for the development of education, the Government of India appointed various educational commissions. In 1956, Sri Prakasa Committee on moral instruction at the primary stage education pointed that how the elementary stage of education influences moral instruction and how these activities should be conducted, and how "school assembly should be held for a few minutes in the morning for group singing"[66].

Those who are involved should be sincere in organising such assemblies. In the primary period moral education should be free from evil environment. The moral instruction should be nursed in the way of good nature. Moral instruction in the elementary stage can be "simple and interesting stories about the lives and teachings of prophets, saints and religious leaders should be included in the syllabus for language teaching"[67]. oral education is also related to religious instruction and religious leaders and saints preached good principles earlier in India and other countries. All the religious principles should be taught in schools but not any one single religion, because in India there are so many co-existing religions like Hinduism, Islam and Christianity. Therefore India needed to be religiously integrated and secular.

Furthermore in the primary stage, moral instruction stresses:

> Wherever possible the interest of the child may also be aroused by the use of audio-visual material, especial good quality photographs, filmstrips and coloured reprint showing great works of the main living religions of the world, such material could be used in the teaching of geography[68].

The modern development of educational technology should be used such as the audio-visual teaching aids for better understanding of the children.

In the school programme, it was noted further by the Prakasham Committee that, two periods a week should be set aside for moral instruction. In these classes, the teacher should relate interesting stories drawn from the great religious men of the world and explain broadly their ethical teachings. Unjust demands and orthodox rituals of religion, which are harmful to the society,[69] should be excluded from moral instruction.

Through school programme, the attitude of 'service' and 'the work is worship' should be developed in the child. "All schemes of physical education and all forms of play in the school contribute to the building of character and in the inculcation of the spirit of true sportsmanship"[70].

Moral instruction is imparted to the children because, 'today's children are tomorrow's citizens'. The future of a nation depends on its good citizens. Education forms the social aspect also aimed at training for good citizenship. Good citizens possess moral conduct. Education should aim at developing a sense of morality in the pupils behaviour in order to be a useful member of society. They should learn to be morally good and respectful as well as obedient, to their elders. This type of moral behaviour leads them to be good citizens of the society.

Morality and Education at the Secondary Level

The position of moral education in the secondary stage should be followed by the methodical and practical approach unlike at the primary stage. In the primary stage of moral instruction there were directions for moral training, those directions are mostly oral practices. Secondary education in the country is the pattern of education for the children of the age group 14-17 years. A national system of Secondary Education was mainly "to establish schools in India on the lines of the public schools in England open to all without distinction of race or creed or caste or social status"[71].

The aims of Indian Public schools "to prepare boys of ability for positions of service and responsibility in all walks of national life"[72]. The secondary education in the Indian Public Schools aimed, to train the children as useful citizens for the national development and train them to develop into their full stature. The main aim of the secondary education was training of the character and developing leadership qualities. "The code of moral conduct set a high premium on truthfulness and fearlessness, and stressed the moral obligation of public service to justify privilege"[73]. The moral education in the secondary stage stressed more on character building. Secondary education therefore played a vital role in the field of education, and aimed at making it qualitative and value oriented. "The secondary stage may provide the higher leadership but if the purpose of that leadership to be translated into effective programmes of work, there must be a large number of persons who have the requisite knowledge, training, and character to carry them out"[74].

Government of India appointed a Commission[75] on the advice of the Central Advisory Board of Education in 1952-53 regarding secondary education under the Chairmanship of Dr. Mudaliar. According to the Commission, secondary education should aim at the development of students' physical, mental and moral skills and abilities for the development of their country. Secondary education should be developed through educational institutions all over the country to train the students as better, effective and democratic citizens. Education is for the training of character to fit the students to participate creatively as citizens in the emerging democratic social order, the improvement of their practical and vocational efficiency so that they may play their part in building up the economic prosperity of their country; and the development of their literary, artistic and cultural interests, which are necessary for self-expression and for the full development of the human personality, without which a living national culture cannot come into being[76].

Moral Studies as Part and Parcel of the Curriculum

The curriculum of secondary education has languages (mother-tongue, foreign language English and national language Hindi) social studies, general science, mathematics, art and music, craft and physical education. In addition to that the "State Governments and educationists have been thinking of doing some systematic work and have made attempts to develop what is called a common syllabus for moral education"[77]. Moral education therefore was planned to be imparted for the development of abilities and skills as well as leadership qualities.

The role of private enterprise in the field of education is, "these organisations maintaining various stages and sectors of educational institutions all over India"[78]. Private enterprise recognises and works for the quantitative and qualitative development of education in various branches of knowledge but as the business enterprises they neglected moral values in education and they manage the institutions with profits of the institutions. Of course educational institutions which are run by private management have played an important role in modern India for the development of technical and professional education.

Religious and Moral Education in post-Independence India aimed to develop the qaualities and attitudes of the children, as"good for the children is good for the society as well"[79]. The importance of religiosus and moral education in the secondary stage is suitable for democratic societyand especially to Indian society. Secondary education can be termed as the nation-building education and needs to maintain good quality and standards. Even primary teachers come from secondary stage education and in this way the secondary education helps to improve primary education as well as the way for the higher education. Thus, secondary stage education should maintain good qualities and moral environment. The moral discipline should be maintained in the schools for the character building. Discipline and character building is possible through the religious instruction, i. e., teachings of the various religious leaders and saints and their autobiographies.

Educational Committees and commissions recommendations are made on religious and moral education based on the directions given in the constitution. The Indian constitution observed that the religious instruction, Article 28 (1) provides, no religious instruction shall be provided in any educational institution wholly maintained out of state funds...[80] Article 28 (2) provides nothing in (1) shall apply to an educational institution which is administered by the state but has been established under any endowment or trust which requires that religious instruction shall be imparted in such institution[81].

The Secondary education commission recommended that the religious instruction for the development of pupils behaviour and character building should be given. "Religious instruction may be given in schools only on a voluntary basis and outside the regular school hours, such instruction being confined to the children of the particular faith concerned and given with consent of the parents and the managements"[82].

Furthermore for the development of moral and religious

education, the Government of India appointed a Committee on religious and moral education in 1959. The Committee opined that the moral values are very important and that to instruct among students for the development of good manners and discipline is necessary. The Committee recommended these moral values for all the stages— primary, secondary and higher. At the secondary stage of instruction, moral education, the Committee instructed that, it should be both methodical and strict for the practitioners. Moral instruction should be taught from the selected literature, sacred or secular.

The Commission recommended that at the secondary stage in schools "the morning assembly should observe two minutes silence followed by readings from the scriptures or great literature of the world or an appropriate address. Community singing should also be encouraged"[83]. The moral instruction to be followed not only from the holy texts but also from other moral texts. Teaching of moral lessons, should be collected from boigraphy, history and mythology, and should be read by pupils, not merely as literature but also as illustrating the moral truths.

> The essential teachings of the great world religions should be studied as part of the curriculum pertaining to social studies and history. Simple texts and stories concerning different religions may be included in the teaching of languages and general reading[84].

Stories may teach morality by enumerating heroic actions showing that moral conduct ensures satisfaction and happiness, descriptions should be judiciously presented.

> One hour a week should be assigned to moral instruction. The teacher should encourage the habit of discussion in his class. Apart from this regular class instruction, suitable speakers may be invited to address the students on moral and spiritual values. Joint celebrations may be organised on the occasion of important festivals of all religions. Knowledge and appreciation of religions other than one's own and respect for their founders, should be encouraged in various ways including essay competitions and declamations[85].

Moral education for secondary stage children commission stated that it helps them to improve their qualities such as self-discipline, love, humanity and character building. A teacher should direct all his efforts towards moulding the character of his pupils through discussing the topics of morality which leads to discipline. "Qualities of character and behaviour of students should form an essential part of the overall assessment of a student's performance at school"[86].

Moral education is connected mainly with religious teaching and also with other branches of knowledge. In fact every religions has moral values but moral principle need not be religious ideals. "Moral education should not be regarded as synonymous with instruction in formal religious principles. ..."[87].

The Commission discussed that secondary stage moral education could be possible through the social studies teaching. These integrated studies should help to teach moral values. The teaching of various religious leaders like Buddha, Jesus, Mohammed and services of the great kings like Ashoka's Dharma, the tenets of Bhakti and Sufi saints are connected with the unit of history in social studies. Lessons on liberty and equality, rights and duties, declaration of American independence, declaration of human rights are related to civics, and equality, emancipation of slaves and the essentials of wants and demand, and the survival of people in their daily life are a few topics in the unit of economics, these units of social studies which can be effectively used to evolve the morality and are necessary for the life of citizens in the society. A moral environment should be favourable in the secondary schools. The moral environment of the children should be made as good exercise as possible. It should be considered in avoiding the extremities of removing the pupils from their home and natural guardian, and serious consideration amidst more favourable surroundings gained by removal from the bad surroundings of the children for the purpose of creating a moral environment in the institutions. Apart from the environment, it should provide in the schools with opportunities to make children in habits of punctuality, obedience to the call of duty, self-restraint and responsibility, all of which are key elements of the code of conduct. Still further it pointed, to physical education in secondary schools. Physical education was introduced in the schools for the purpose of making healthy individuals capable of physical endurance. Training of physical education not only for the physical endurance but also it will mould the behaviours and attitudes through participation in various activities like "scouts and guides", and games. These activities also help them to be sportive and mutual understanding and cooperative manners. "In the post-Independence period, a good deal of expansion of place in the field of education, but all this was at the expanse of quality"[88]. The expansion of qualitative education in India appears to be with absence of values. Especially moral values are neglected in practice in every educational institute in the country. In this connection it should not be called a qualitative expansion of education. Without having instruction of values in education, it could not be considered the qualitative expansion of education. Sri Prakasa Committee (1959) was appointed by the Government of India regarding religious and moral instruction, but the Committee gave less importance to moral instructions.

For the development of education in India the Government of India passed the resolutions through Indian Education Commission (1964-66). It is popularly known as Kothari Commission. The Commission stated that, "The destiny of India is now being shaped in her classrooms"[89]. The Commission gave priority for educational programmes to reach national goals through following four-fold path:

1. Education is related to productivity;
2. Strengthens social and national integration; consolidates democracy as a form of Government and helps the country to adopt it as a way of life;
3. Hastens the process of Modernization; and
4. Strives to build character by cultivating social, moral and spiritual values[90].

Thus, the Commission recommended that the development of education should be on national pattern in India. It advocated for science education in all stages of education. The Commission recommended that the programme of education should be related to productivity. It recognised the importance of vocational courses in secondary education. Thus the Education Commission gave importance to the social and national services and co-curricular activities should be imparted in all stages of education. It could be considered that the social and national services should be regarded as moral obligations and a sense of self-respect and moral responsibility should be developed among the students.

Furthermore the Commission recommended the moral and religious education.

"Conscious and organised attempts be made for imparting education in social, moral and spiritual be made for imparting education in social, moral and ethical teachings of great religions"[91]. Thus the Commission recognised that the moral instruction was necessary in educational institutions and that it was the ultimate aim of education.

> All education in a way is a moral process but special efforts in the present social climate showing a decline in our values are necessary it would be ideal to have two periods per month, two should be devoted to some kind of project which would instal in children a love for the service of others and specially of the disabled and the needy[92].

Thus, secondary education is most important for the development of education and is the gateway of university education. The most important objectives of secondary education are related with the values.

Pupils development through instruction in schools is to bring them a balanced development of the personality of their mind, body and soul through an ideal life of virtue, purity, goodness, selfcontrol, self-discipline, kindness, service, courage and idealism, fulfilment of one's duties and responsibilities, make for developing qualities of good citizenship[93].

Morality and Education at Higher Level

Before Independence so many Universities were established in India for the development of economic, social, political and cultural values. In the post-Independence India, education assumed a very significant place in human life. After Independence the Indian Government had appointed the

University Education Commission (1948-49)[94] for the development of University education. The Commission dealt with the improvement of length and content of courses and standards related with teaching and research and terms and conditions as a whole.

Moral Education as Part and Parcel of Curriculum

In the post-Independence era, Higher Education has many aims and objective for the development of the nation. The Government of India and its leaders, aspired to have the economic, social, political situations to be improved in the country through education.

Modern Indian Policy on education aimed that education should change the evil conditions of the country. Especially higher education should be used for the development of literary, scientific, technical abilities and skills of the people, to fulfill the needs and aspirations of the country.

"It is for the Universities to create knowledge and train minds who would bring together the two-material resources and human energies"[95]. All these changes should improve the spirit of the people to live in better conditions.

Thus, another aim of education to be considered is the education for the development of individuality. the object of education is to give men or women the unity of truth, the fullest growth and freedom of self, in order to maintain self-respect which we owe to ourselves, to others and to the creator.

An important aim of the Higher Education in modern India is, training for leadership. Through instruction, the qualities and responsibilities of the social life can be developed among the students. The University Commission observed that in education, training for leadership "to know the nature and consequences of ethical values, to sense the meaning of social forces operating in the world today and comprehend the complexities and intricacies of life in all its immensity, physical, social and spiritual"[96]. The importance of the training for leaderships is to develop the persons abilities in various fields of knowledge. "The quantity of civilization depends not on the material equipment or the political machinery but on the character of men. The major task of education is the improvement of character"[97].

Thus, the chief aim of higher education in modern India is love for higher values of life. In the matter of higher education, the function of a University, consists of acquiring, disseminating and extending knowledge including promotion of human values, competencies and cultural excellences with those of other cultures, facilitating national unity and growth through the national outlook. The totality of personality developing through education among its members, and promoting communication abilities of the persons. Higher education in the country should help to change the attitudes and beliefs of the students, teachers and others of the educational institutions.

> Our Universities must educate on the right lines and provide proper facilities for educating a large number of people. If we do not have the necessary intelligence and ability to work but these purposes, we must get them through the Universities[98].

Education as its aim, should also create an integrated personality. The education must aim to awaken people, to develop a sense of integrity. Education should promote the sense of social and national consciousness and it is open to all irrespective of caste, creed, religion, community and economic status.

Education should be aimed to national integration and this to be extended for the international understanding. Evidently, in the freedom struggle and the sacrifices that the people had made for attaining Independence, must become an essential part of the curriculum at all stages of education. It is necessary to improve a core content with the purpose of the students in different parts of the country with the struggle and the sacrifices that the country had made for achieving Independence. So the sense of unity and integrity be developed as a fundamental element of education. The integrated mind would develop in the individual a social responsibility for the people and the country. These values and responsibilities help to develop humanism in the minds and lives of the people :

> A University stands for humanism, for tolerance for reason, for the adventure of ideas and search for the truth. It stands for the onward march of the human reach towards even higher objectives. If the Universities discharge their duties adequately, then it is well with the nation and the people[99].

Integrated development of human sense in the youth would help to broaden the understanding of life and do service to the humanity.

In Democratic India, the growing decay of morality among Indian youth has necessiated moral and religious education in all institutions. Therefore, democratic values are imparted to students at the national level. The preamble to the constitution gives to the people equal opportunity without any discrimination.

> On the Indian Republic-Devolves the task of harmonizing the French passion for liberty, the British genius for Government by discussion and reasoned opposition, and the American insistence on the supermacy of the law, as well as the Indian Dharma (Religion) concept as our ultimate guide and sanction. The recognition of a need for investigation and for tolerance of vergant points of view earliest time down to the age of Sankara and Ramanuja, should stand us in good stead in that hormonization of paralleled ideals, which has been attempted by our legislators and which must become part of our political and intellectual consciousness[100].

Thus the idea of democratic principles of 'liberty, equality and fraternity' are the highest principles of universal utilitarianism. Widely, the good of all, is the one ideal aim of ethical practice.

The position of moral and religious education at the University stage has been noted from the recommendations of the University Commission, and Sri Prakasa Committee. The ultimate aim of education is concerned with moral values, particularly the conduct of man. Moral instruction is for the development of the moral sense among the students. It considered as "the individual experience and growth by which the capacity to distinguish between standards of right and wrong is gradually achieved and become progressively influential in the individual's social behaviour"[101].

The Moral instruction in higher educational institutions or Universities is imparted for the development of values in education. "A University is a place where people go in search of knowledge and wisdom, ideals and values and we should expect the alumni to be engaged in the serious task of pursuing knowledge, and imbibing right values"[102].

Moral education in University should be more systematic than that during the pre-higher stage. If the instruction of moral culture is neglected, then the higher intellectual culture will fail to make a real contribution to the society. The importance of moral education is much greater than that intellectual education and the purpose of moral instruction is to eliminate the defective evils and construct good habits, good manners and behaviour.

In the University, students should be encouraged to meet in groups for silent meditation in the mornings. These meetings shall be supervised by the staff members on a voluntary basis.

A general study of different religions should be an essential part of the general education course in degree classes. In this connection, points of the University education Commission had the following.

In the first year of the degree course, lives of the great religious and spiritual leaders like Gautama the Buddha, Confucious, Zoraster, Socrates, Jesus, Shankara, Ramanuja, Madhava, Mohammad, Kabir, Nanak and Gandhi be taught.

In the second year, some selections of a Universal character from the scriptures of the world be studied, and that in the third year, the central problem of philosophy of religion be considered. Standard works for such studies should be prepared carefully by specialists who have deep knowledge and sympathy for the religious systems.

A post-graduate course in comparative religion may be instituted. Due importance should be given to the study of the following subjects in the appropriate Honours and M. A. courses in the fields of Humanities and social Sciences. Comparitive Religion and History of Religion:

> A fairly long period of social service should be introduced by all Universities. In the organisation and conduct of such service,

> considerable attention should be given to the learning and practice of moral and spiritual values[103].

In this regard the systematic moral instruction should be followed by methods of teaching. Particularly the moral teaching for higher level has theoretical and practical method of teaching. The theoretical method for desirable teaching to take place, the doctrines should be arranged according to some method to be inculcated. It should maintain determining of right and wrong, it does not mean a regular course of teaching on ethics, and it should involve the discussion of many critical matters, such as the question of free will and necessity. Thus, there should be some important facts to be provided in theoretical moral instruction and the person who has to teach must have a sense for distinguishing between right and wrong and he should be able to defend the distinction between what is right is good and what is wrong is evil. Self-determination is the key part of the moral progress, and it should be attained. Every Human being should be taught moral values.

From practical moral teaching, the teacher should inculcate the principles of truth, and right actions, etc., like telling the truth in day to day life; avoid giving pain to any one; learn to do anything with right thinking and its consequences; practice to do the right actions.

Every one should be trained to avoid doing harm and selfishness, as well as the sense of destroying other's property. Examine the acts and omit the one which brought bad results. Self-examination is the best scrutiny in daily life. Everybody should have faith in the operation of moral laws and should entertain the true notion which is good. The above stated aims are possible to train by practical approach.

The system of higher education in modern India, is in need of exphasis on morals in education in our college, it is not easy to frame a curriculum in education[104]. Actually, the students "in their homes and largely influenced by their parents where the seeds of true morality are deeply sown"[105]. Colleges should prescribe for the students some important books for reading as supplementary and other publications bearing moral values such as character building, self-respect, universal brotherhood, etc. They should be taught secular, democratic and religious values. Therefore every college library should have sufficient books related with all great men of social, religious leaders who had good character and high moral lives. It is true that the maintenance of the books in libraries does not solve the problem as the students are not interested in reading the books. The students that, many educational institutions and Universities are facing problems because of lack of morality.

In modern India, the Indian Education Commission (1964-66) was appointed for the defusion of education on national pattern. It suggested that in the Universities;

> their principal object is to deepen man's understanding of the universe and of himself in body, mind and spirit, to disseminate this understanding throughout society and to apply it in the service of mankind. They are the dwelling places of ideas and ideals, integrity from all their members. Their's is the pursuit of truth and excellence in all its diversity a pursuit which needs above all, courage, and fearlessness[106].

It considers a moral obligation to higher education.

The system of University or higher education has important responsibilities to maintain the balanced education in the society. Higher Values of individuals. The system and functions of the Universities should have several points as follows:

— inculcate and promote basic human values and the capacity to choose between alternative value system;

— Preserve and foster our great cultural traditions and blend them with essential elements from other cultures and peoples;

— Promote a rational outlook and scientific temper;

— Enrich the Indian languages and promote their use as important means of communication, national development and unity;

— Promote the development of the total personality of the students and inculcate in them a commitment to society through involvement in national service programme;

— Act as an objective critic of society and assist in the formulation of national objectives and programmes for their realisation;

— Promote commitment to the pursuit of excellence;

— Promote the development of science and technology and of an indigenous capability to apply it effectively with special emphasis on national problems : on above all;

— Contribute to the improvement of the entire educational system so as to subserve the community[107].

Therefore in all the stages of education in modern India ultimately aspired to achieve the ultimate aim of education which deals with social and moral values to be imparted and those which are stressed through various commissions and committees related in the field of education. But in a practical approach, especially moral education is deteriorating at the University stage. In fact, the University stage should have high values. In modern India, moral values in education are in a declining position from the lower to higher levels. In fact from the primary stages to higher stages, education should impart moral values in an ascending order to the students. All the committees and commissions related with education in modern India perceived the importance of moral instruction and the lack of it. But the recommendations of the committees and commission on moral instruction have faild in implementation for several reasons.

It is taken here into consideration the instrucation of moral values in education as a subject as well as part of other subjects in the institutions. Because the moral values like discipline, character building, skillfulness, etc., are important as objectives of education. These values are take place in instrucation through the required curriculum and syllabus at all the stages of education. The instrucation of the other subjects especially languages and Humanities are also useful as important vehicle to develop such values in education. For each subject or discipline should try to develop it's own skills and abilities, so that the sense of skills characterise the moral sense among learners but it depends on the ability of the teacher.

Every subject has to try, to define the moral values. The Humanities such as history, civics or politics, economics mainly deal with facts and realities of the social life. For the matter of higher education, philosophy, sociology, and above mentioned subjects also relate with day to day life of Human beings and they were closely connected with human ideas and ideals of moral and cultural values. Therefore, students should cultivate in their life, the skills associated with social and human values, as well as moral skill and abilities. the ethical and social skills lead to the good life of the community. They are abtained through the practice of truthfulness, honesty, understanding of social awareness, self-examination, non-violence, right action, pure love, etc.

References

1. B. N. Luniya, *Indian Heritage and Culture,* Lakshmi Narain Agarwal Agra, 11th. edition, 1990, p. 422.
2. B. N. Luniya, *Op. cit.,* p. 423.
3. S. N. Mukherji, *An Introduction to Indian Education,* p. 2.
4. *Idem.*
5. B. N. Luniya, *Op. cit.,* p. 425.
6. N. N. Law, *Promotion of Learning in India by Early European Seltens,* pp. 7-8.
7. W. H. Sharp, *Selections from Educational Records,* Vol. 1, p. 3.
8. S. N. Mukherji, *Op. cit.,* p. 2.
9. J. P. Naik and Syed Nurullah, *A Students History of Education in India (1800-1973),* p. 57.
10. R. G. Wilder, *Mission Schools in India,* pp. 36-37, quoted J. P. Naik and S. Nurullah, *A Students History of Education in India (1800-1973),* pp. 38-39.
11. Herry Sharp, ed, *Selections from education records,* Quoted by K. Kalyan, Chatterjee, *English Education in India,* issues and opinions, The Macmillan Company of India Ltd., Delhi, 1976, p. 11.
12. Report of the select Committee of the House of Commons on the affairs of the East India Company (1832),

Appendix 1, pp. 325-327, quoted B. P. Singh, *Aims and Education in India,* p. 107.

13. J. P. Naik, *Educational Planning in India,* p. 67.
14. Kalyan K. Chatterjee, *English Education in India, issues and opinions,* p. 100.
15. Lord Curzon in India, Vol. II, p. 54, quoted J. P. Naik and S. Nurullah, *A Student's History of Education in India,* p. 266.
16. *Educational documents in India (1831-1968),* ed. by B. D. Bhatt and J. C. Agarwal, p. 26.
17. *Ibid.*
18. *Adam's Report,* Calcutta Edition, pp. 349-50, quoted J. P. Naik, *Op. cit.*
19. Woods Despatch - Para 77, quoted J. P. Naik and S. Nurullah, *A Students History of Education in India (1800-1973),* p. 143.
20. J. P. Naik, *Educational Planning in India,* Allied Publishers, Delhi, 1965, p. 66.
21. Kalyan K. Chatterjee. *English Education in India,* p. 40.
22. *Ibid.*
23. S. N. Mukherji, *History of Education in India (Modern period),* Acharya Book Depot, Baroda, p. 75.
24. Kalyan K. Chatterjee, *Op. cit.,* p. 41.
25. Kalyan K. Chatterjee, *Op. cit.,* p. 41.
26. S. N. Mukherji, *Op. cit.,* p. 35.
27. *Ibid,* p. 48.
28. S. N. Mukherji, *Op. cit.,* p. 49.
29. *Ibid,* p. 146.
30. J. P. Naik, *Educational Planning in India,* p. 67.
31. S. N. Mukherji, *Op. cit.,* p. 164.
32. *Hunter Commission Report,* quoted S. N. Mukherji, *Op. cit.,* p. 167.
33. *Ibid,* p. 168.
34. *Sadler Commission Report,* p. 219.
35. *Hartog Committee Report,* p. 235.

36. B. C. Rai, *History of Education,* Prakasam Kendra, Lucknow, 1991, p. 143.
37. Resolution on Educational Policy (1904) quoted J. P. Naik and S. Nurullah, *A Students History of Education in India,* p. 366.
38. S. N. Mukherji, *Op. cit.,* p. 98.
39. *Ibid,* p. 135.
40. S. N. Mukherji, *Op. cit.,* p. 135.
41. Wood's Despatch, *Quoted in Educational Documents in India (1813-1968),* ed. B. D. Bhatt and J. C. Aggarwal, p. 6.
42. S. N. Mukherji, *Op. cit.,* p. 135.
43. Macaulay's Minutes (1835). *Selections from education records,* Part 1, pp. 107-117, K. S. Vakil and S. Natarajan, *Education in India,* p. 113.
44. Kalyan K. Chatterjee, *English Education in India,* p. 99.
45. J. P. Naik and S. Nurullah, *A Students History of Education in India,* pp. 202-203.
46. Hunter Commission, 1882; *Report of the Indian Education Commission,* p. 18.
47. J.P. Naik and S. Nurullah, *Op. cit.,* p. 366.
48. K. K. Chatterji, *Op. cit.,* p. 109.
49. Quoted Kalyan K. Chatterjee, *English Education in India,* p. 59.
50. Kalyan K. Chatterjee, *Op. cit.,* p. 116.
51 Kalyan K. Chatterjee, *Op. cit.,* p. 116.
52. Shri R. V. Parulekar, quoted J. P. Naik, *A Students History of Education in India,* p. 11.
53. *Hunter Commission Report,* 1882. *Op. cit.,* p. 39.
54. R. V. Parulekar, Curzon's Reforms, British India Gazetts, *Archives of India,* p. 215.
55. Jagannath Mohanty, *Education in India,* Deep & Deep Publications, New Delhi, 1987, p. 38.
56. Raghunath sofia, *The Educational Review, Madras,* p. 9.
57. G.T. Terry Page and J.B. Thomas with A.R. Marshal, *International Dictionary of Education (London),* p. 627, Requoted from Sita Rama Sharma : *Education in India,* Anmol Publications, New Delhi, p.3.

58. J. Mafitain, *Education at the Crossroads,* p.10, Oxford University Press, London, 1914.
59. Roussoue quoted by : Raghunath Safia, *The Educational Review,* Sept., 1991, Vol. x CVII, p. 9.
60. M.K. Gandhi, *Basic Education,* p. 11.
61. M.K. Gandhi, *To the Students,* p. 14.
62. Government of India, Planning commission, the First Five Year Plan, p. 531. Quoted Sita Rama Sharma, *Education in India,* p. 145.
63. M.K. Gandhi, *Basic Education* (1951), p. 51, quoted in Dhurjati Mukherjee, *The Towering Spirit,* Gandhian relevance assessed, New Delhi, Chetan Publications, 1978, p. 86.
64. G.D. Benerjee, *A Few Thoughts on Education,* S.K. Lahiri & Co., Cotton Press, Calcutta, 1910, p. 17.
65. *Idid,* p. 18.
66. Sri Prakasa Committee : *The Committee on Religious and Moral Instruction,* 1959. NCERT (Pub.) Documents on social, moral and spiritual values in Education, p. 20.
67. Sri Prakasa Committee, NCERT (Pub.), *Opcit.,* p. 20
68. Idem.
69. Sri Prakasa Committee, NCERT (Pub.), *Opcit.,* p. 20.
70. Alfred De Souja, *Indian Public Schools - A Sociological Study,* p. 23.
71. Sri Prakasa committee, *NCERT (Pub),* Op. cit., p. 20.
72. Alfred De Souja, *Op.cit.,* p. 27.
73. *Ibid,* p. 52.
74. Humayun Kabir, *Education in New India,* p. 40.
75. *Mudaliar Commission on Secondary Education in Inida,* 1952-53.
76. *Mudaliar Commission's Report,* p. 24.
77. G.N. Kaul, *Values and Education in Independent India,* The Associated Publishers, Ambala, p. 45.
78. J.C. Aggarwal and S.P. Aggarwal, *Educational Planning in India,* with a slant to educational financing and administration, p. 70.

79. Humayun Kabir, *Education in New India,* p. 39.
80. Indian Constitution, Article 28 (1) and (2).
81. J.C. Aggarwal, *Development and Planning of Modern Education,* p. 110.
82. Secondary Education Commission, 1952-53. *Quoted in Documents on Social, Moral and Spiritual Values in Educaton* (1979), p. 13.
83. Sri Prakasa Committee, 1959. NCERT (Pub), *Documents on Social, Moral and Spiritual Values in Education,* 1979, p. 21.
84. Idem.
85. Sri Prakasa Committee, NCERT (Pub), *Op. cit.,* p. 21.
86. *Idem.*
87. B.W. Heath, *Religious Education and Primary Teacher,* p. 6; quoted V.S. Madhyastha, *Journal of Indian Education,* May 1978, p. 30.
88. J.C. Aggarwal, *Development and Planning of Modern Education (1982),* p. 118.
89. *Education Commission,* 1964-66 (1.01), p. 1; *Education Commission in India,* p. 225.
90. *Education Commission,* 1964-66 (1.20), p. 6

    *Educational Documents in India,*p. 256.
91. J.C. Aggarwal, *Development and Planning of Mordern Education,* p. 125.
92. Education Commission, 1964-66, *Educational Documents in India,* pp. 284-285.
93. Ibid, p. 286.
94. University Education Commission, 1948-49, Government in India.
95. University Education Commission, Education Documents in India, p. 98.
96. B.D. Bhatt and J.C. Aggarwal, *Educational Documents in India,* p. 102.
97. B.D. Bhatt and J.C. Aggarwal, *Educational Documents in India,* pp. 102-103.
98. *Ibid,* p. 101
99. Jawaharlal Nehru, *In his convocation address to the University of Allahabad,* 1947.

100. C.P. Iyer, *"The Republic Ideal"* Reported in the Hindustan Times Republic Day, Special Number, January 26, 1950, New Delhi.

101. Catter V. Good (ed), *Dictionary of Education,* (New York, McGraw Hill Company, 1959, p. 167).

102. K.L. Shrimali, *A Search for Values in India Education,* p. 36.

103. University Eduaction Commission, 1948-49, B.D. Bhatt and J.C. Aggarwal, *Op. cit.,* pp. 209-210.

104. M.S. Venkatachari, *The Educational Review (Madras),* May, 1992, p. 98.

105. *Idem.*

106. B.D. Bhatt and J.C. Aggarwal, *Educational Documents in India,* p. 265.

107. J. C. Aggarwal, *Development and Planning of Modern Education with Special Reference to India,* pp. 230-231.

5

Immorality and Modern Indian Education

We need a system of education which will aim at producing the whole man, the complete man who shall not use his theoretical knowledge for destructive purposes. Who shall always utilise his knowledge and not suffer from the daulity of beguilling language and empty character.

R.N. Vyas, Education at the Cross Roads

Modern Indian educational institutions, especially higher institutions, are facing a moral crisis. The number and intensity of incidences of immorality are increasing rapidly. Incidences like violence, arson, cheating, malpractices, etc. Performance of such actions are not restricted to the student population alone, as teachers and administrators are also involving themselves more and more, when compared to other periods of education.

Before the situation goes completely out of hand because to a large extent it already has the marks of it those who are responsible for the smooth running and progress of it must take immediate action of putting an end to such incidences, or at least reducing them considerably. The danger a nation has to face is handing itself over to the hands of its untrustworthy, insincere, inhuman and anti-human youth; they become the weakness of the nation instead of its strength. In a broader sense, they are the product of nation, through its educational institutions. Therefore, India, as a nation has to feel the responsibility in rectifying the situation taking strong remedial measures. No doubt the problem, if left to itself would engulf the entire structure and the main purpose of education. It is high time to take real note of these causes, with those people who are guilty, either directly or indirectly, and to take necessary actions against them in an academic and legal way.

It is important to make a note in this context that, it is easy to gather the types of problems and their causes, but to find out the real causes, deeper and indirect, is a tougher job. But the work of indicating remedial measures, which are not utopian. of course, if there is no sincere effort on the part of responsible persons in whose hands the process of rectification lies every remedial measure to be unpracticable.

This chapter deals with the problems concerned with immorality of the students, teachers and administrators in the modern educational institutions and some causes of and remedies for those problems.

Everyday the printed media, the radio and the television, show increasing of corrupt practices in public life, religious and communal conflicts, terrorist activities, etc. Though they may seem to be sporadic incidents unconcerned with the educational institutions, every institution in the society, more so, the modern educational institutions, are mostly concerned or responsible. One cannot undrmine the role the educational institutions can play in moulding the character of the youth.

It is to be noted that the problems are created mostly by the terrorists. Most of the corrupt practices in the offices are undoubtedly by the educated and even educated politicians are not above board. Those are the deviants from moral rules and values. In this connection it must be stressed that "at present, education produces an incomplete man"[1]. Many educationists and those who are mostly concerned with education, hold the same view about modern education and the urgent need of rectifying its defects.

> We need a system of education which will aim at producing the whole man, the complete man who shall not use his theoretical knowledge for destructive purposes. Who shall always utilise his knowledge and energy for the welfare of entire humanity, who shall not suffer from the duality of beguilling language and empty character[2].

Moral values are needed through educatin must be built by the lives of the students mainly and thereby the existing problems can be rectified. The development of a country is based largely on the system of education. Education must give importance to moral development of the individuals. It should not neglect the aims, such as character building, all-round development, cultivating finer senses, and humanness of the individual, Gandhi, who stresses on character says : "... what we need, what any nation need, but we perhaps, of all the nations of the world, need just now, is nothing else and nothing less than character building"[3].

Gandhi believed that the character of the individual is to be measured by the completeness of the person. In addition to this he says "we would deserve nothing unless we had character to back what we wish for"[4].

There is the need of proper understanding and concern for the problems arising out of devation, from moral values, in the modern educational institutions. The development of education is quantitatively satisfactory, but not qualitatively. It is not a value oriented education. Gandhi wanted Indian youth to be trained for the highest ideals of life to build a society founded on self-discipline, love and service and everyone to fulfill his duties.

Modern Indian education is neglecting "basic qualities as compassion, endurance, courage... truthfulness, faithfulness, lovalty to do duty and the common good".[5] Modern education gives importance to scientific and technological development than development of moral values. "The current trends are a product of the scientifc revolution followed by the industrial revolution, ushering in the technocratic age and culminating in a cultural crises"[6].

Modern society is craves immediate benefits and materialistic advancement and so the youth is being attracted undermining the real values in life. Generally, education reflects the process of cultural, social, economic and industrial changes and thereby values change from time to time. Education is neglecting the basic moral values. "Technological progress has created a dangerous situation—a cultural lag—making this age an age of demolition and not reconstruction"[7].

Generally, formal education is given through institutions and they are a network of the students, teachers and administrators. Moral problems in educational institutions pertain to such a network.

SECTION-I

Students' Misbehaviour Problems : Some Causes and Remedies

> The children now love luxury. They have bad manners, contempt for authority. They show disrespect for their elders and love chatter in place of exercise. They no longer rise when elders enter the room. They contradict their parents, chatter before company, rattle dishes at the table, cross their legs and tyrannize over their teachers.

The words of socrates, quoted by J.A. Battle and Robert L. Shannon, *The New Idea in Education*

Present Position of the Educational Institutions

The disciplinary conditions in modern Indian Educational institutions is out of hand. Strikes, gheraos, and fighting for unjust causes, violence, sometimes going to the extent of man-handling the students, teachers and administrators, malpractices in the examination halls; threatening the invigilators and evaluators; atrocities at the time of student union elections; owning the library books, i.e., stealing, group fightings, inhabituated to lying freely. These are acting against the norms and code of decent behaviour. "we hear of violence and destruction of public property indulged in more by University and college students than by other categories of the population"[8].

All these problems are concerned with the students, and the sad fact is, the percentage of such behaviour and incidents are in ascending order from day to day. If this is allowed to happen, what would be the fate of the youth, institutions and the commumity in the future.

Students in modern times are specimens of failures in educatinal institutions, because they are not truly getting educated. They are simply trained to pass examinatins for certificates and degrees only. These institutions have become workshops to pruduce degree holdrs. about the true nature of the educational institution:

> Maintenance of moral standard among students is inherent in the very idea of educaton. The reputation of an institution is not a mere commercial asset depending on the length and duration of its existence. An educational institution worth its name should have its purpose the improvement of the moral and intellectual standards of its students. On the contrary, laxity in such encorcement will defeat the very purpose of the institution and will bring into disrepute[9].

Modern educational institutions, especially in private management are more concerned with profit making, than turning out really educated youth. The teaching methods that are being adopted are exam-oriented rather than subject-oriented and value-oriented. Both the public and private maintenance of institutions are facing student problems, because of lack of maintenance of proper discipline and not cultivating values in the life of its student population.

The word discipline has been derived from the Latin root 'disciplus' meaning pupil or disciple. The word literally means"...the process of learning and training which is for some ends. Discipline has wide significance in education"[10]. The modern sense of discipline is according to Makkar:

> The training of mind, attitudes and good manners as well as development of character. Thus, the discipline helps the person for the development of good habits and attitudes. It is positive, constructive, creative and self-willed[11].

The term 'indiscipline' has been defined as untrained mind and wrong attitude. It is sometimes make a narrow sense and clumsy.

Classroom Situation

In formal education, teaching at all levels takes place between the teacher and the taught and within the institution. Normally, teaching activity is performed in a classroom. A class is a group or collection of individuals, i.e., the teacher and students. A classroom is more than an accommodation for the teacher and students and a class is more than a collection of teacher and students. It is a congenial ground for sowing the seeds of knowledge.

Classroom plays an important role in moulding the students, it being a basic part of modern education systems it should be physically good and should be properly maintained. Because it is occupied and shared collectively by a group of students, a set of rules and regulations are imposed by the management for disciplined and proper conduct of classes. Classroom rules offer the best opportunity for involvement and commitment. "They are the most readily altered and responsive to the needs of the students"[12].

In the classroom, students develop their knowledge and skills as well as behaviour. They cooperate with each other, in classroom activities as well as outside of it.

Although the rules and norms are imposed by the teacher or organisation in the classroom and school for the development of the student, sometimes they feel inconvenient with rules and they treat them as restrictions on their freedom (from the point of:) in this regard, A. Krat stated:

> All too often rules are handed out 'cold'. Students are given a bunch of regulations orally or in pamphlet form in which the key words repeated over and over 'no' and 'don't'. Students are apt to perceive rules so issued as restrictions on their freedom[13].

In modern educational institutions classroom is packed with students' misbehaviour. "We shall treat indiscipline and misconduct as one and the same and consider unfair means as a part of indiscipline or misconduct"[14].

All the negative activities and expressions of the students are considered as misbehaviour. Behavioural aspects of the students like, friendliness, cohessiveness, righteousness, love and cooperation with each other, etc., constitute positive expressions of behaviour. But in modern educational institutions students lack the positive aspect of behaviour. The teacher orders the students in the learning-teaching situation in the classroom,"...how to behave, what to do or not to do, most often so that the class can continue its work"[15]. The teacher ordering like 'sit-down-and-shut-up' is not at all harmful and it is not an 'insult' or 'innuendo' to the students. But, the modern students feel"... squashed and can either conform or rebel-overtly or covertly"[16].

The students' misbehaviour it considered the students are consequently forget the rules and they conform"...sheepishly, anxiously, or resentfully or violate them when the occasion arises"[17]. With all these reasons, the classroom is disturbed. In fact, students' disciplined behaviour in all respects lead them to attain goals and they make inter-relationship with each other.

The main aims and objectives of the classroom are improvement of learning-teaching activity, in imparting knowledge and skills. But, misbehaviour of the students vitiate the classroom atmosphere and its purposes. Consequently, the subjects and skills as well as moral values deteriorate in educational institutions. Immorality, irregularity, wasting of time, unfaithfulness, rivalry, hardness, misunderstanding and disobedience, etc., are considered as students' misbehaviour in the classroom.

Students personal interests and desires are some of the causes of moral problems in educational institutions. The modern students interests are influenced by social and cultural changes mainly on scientific and technological development. Modern man is being attracted by the immediate material benefits. Generally human interests are concerned with desire and enjoyment, material or immaterial.

But modern youth's interests are selfish and restricted to materialistic enjoyments. They want immediate fruits but have no desire for practice of 'Dharma' and 'Moksha'. The members of such group are more concerned about 'life-oriented' roles rather than 'career-oriented' or 'value-oriented' goals. The unwanted exposer to outside the classroom and institutional activities of the students are a cause of indiscipline in the classroom. According to Tiwari:

> A student today spends much less time in school and is exposed to several other influences which are certainly more educative. He is in touch with the political activities and politicians who keep him aware of the problems of society. He is exposed to films and activities on the streets[18].

Therefore, disciplinary codes or principles are designed to improve student awareness, "...moral principles are imposed among students in the learning process to mould their behaviour and character development is called discipline"[19].

Reasons for these problems are lack of playgrounds in schools and on the other hand teachers concentrate on their personal work and involvment in other affairs than school or college work.

"Therefore, classroom atmosphere should be maintained for group interaction...friends; others to trust and turn to, others who accept, appreciate, care, help, and need one, with whom are 'belongs' /involvement with others/attention from others"[20]. For the purpose of receiving knowledge and developing habits, attitudes and values, to lead a moral life, of the students.

Thus, the classroom experiences primarily oriented to the all-round development of the students, to cultivate in them habits like punctuality, cooperation, team spirit, cohesiveness, responsibility and kind nature in their activities. All of those activities and attitudes for the purpose of maintaining and environment of order and discipline. Thus, the classroom climate should help the students in both academic and moral achievement.

Subject Matter of Education

Students problems are also concerned with the subjects which are prescribed in the institutions. There are many subjects introduced at all stages of education. At the college level there are some subjects which are common for all students and some subjects which are specializations, on the other hand, science and technology has specializations, for science and technical students. At the University level each subject carries as a branch or department.

Modern education provides Humanities, Social Sciences, Languages, Commerce and Management, Law, Science and Technology. And other advanced courses are introduced as specializations in each concerned branch.

Languages are helpful in communicating and they are spread by the people through words, sounds and phenomenal images. Languages improve students' abilities basic skills, and literary communications. All the subjects in the curriculum of an institution depend on the languages to communicate with students. So languages are imparted to every student in an institution.

In all stages of education students face problems in their subjects. All the subjects give the knowledge and skills necessary and produce more and more degrees for the educated. But the problem is that modern students are more concerned with degrees but not subjects. Consequently, most of the students are not paying attention and so are unable to understand the subjects.

The problem with subjects at higher levels of education, is that the subjects are offered on the basis of marks attained by the students and not on their choice. Some students who are interested in some subjects may not get seats because, of lack of sufficient marks, and become frustrated. There is no problem with the merit students in this regard. But the remaining students who join in the graduate or post-graduate courses without any interest in the subject, do not pay any attention to the lessons.

The reasons for the negligence of value-orientation in education are a misunderstanding of it by the students, teachers and administrators, and lack of control and discipline. In this regard:

> The crisis of value is caused by the weakening and neglect of the ethical, moral and spiritual dimensions of man's nature and his existences. The role and contribution of education must be fully and imaginatively directed to the solution of

> this basic problem of our time. Many other world problems confronting mankind are related to this crisis of values[21].

At all levels in educational institutions there are subjects contributing values for social purpose. In the teaching-learning process, these values have disappeared because the method of instruction is not so much involved with values. Modern educational methods are used to motivate students on the subject matter, but not on values.

The branches of knowledge and scientific-technological developments are there in modern societies. But in terms of moral values, they are not even developing science and technology created a more prosperous and in the world as a whole. Consequently, the concept of moral problems are also created by technological affluences, and maladies of social, economic and political incidents and involvement.

Generally, traditional values, had for so many centuries upheld the home, the temple, church and the community. But in modern society, "the responsibility of education has now shifted from the family, religious institutions, subsidised schools and apprentice guides to public authorities and the state"[22]. Education is more misguided with political interference. Therefore, education is not in a position to achieve its real aims due to its lack of a good academic and moral atmosphere in the educational institutions. Students are paying less attention to the subjects while taught. Because, there is lack of control or discipline. The students do not involve themselves in the learning process in understanding the subjects, but they enjoy their indisciplinary activities. The relationship depends on psychological development. Psychologically underdeveloped or developing students are involved in the 'Disruptive Behaviour'.

There are other problems with subjects particularly in higher education. Students in subjects like Humanities, Languages, Social Sciences are most unconcerned with 'occupations'. Generally higher education should be interrelated with occupation and the subject. For instance, there is relevance between subject and occupation in science and technology. But the languages, Humanities and social sciences in modern education have no relevance to the occupations in the community. (Some professional courses exempted from this idea). In this regard, students in higher education have less involvement in the subject matter. All these reasons lead to disruptive behaviour and the indiscipline of the students in educational institutions.

The following are the remedies to rectify the problems involved in classroom situations and the subjects. Moral values are inherent and intrinsic. While teaching the subjects in educational institutions the teacher can give more stress directly or indirectly to moral values. A hierarchy of value system in education is essential and students must learn that, moral values should have primacy over other systems of values regarding the economy, politics, social organisations and so on. Teaching the subjects, especially, social studies or Humanities should be aimed to train the students in social and moral values like 'Honesty', and 'cooperation', etc.

Subjects in educational institutions should be provided with a good deal of value orientation for the students. To teach various subjects the institutions should have good administration and teachers, to create an ethical environment in the campus. If students have to attain real values through education, and have to carry on real virtues against immorality, education should begin with primary and secondary levels and teach moral values.

Thus, the subjects should be taught for the all-round development of students. So, moral education should be imparted to all students. And that should include the development of knowledge, self-respect and attitudes for the realization of a humane and virtuous life. It should aim at eliminating indiscipline and promoting character-development. Every student must have moral qualities and attitudes for becoming real humans in the society. Every institution should create a moral environment, to appreciate and adopt moral values. "Virtue, character and discipline are of real worth only when they stand firm in the actual world of daily work, temptation and trial, and bear the wear and tear of ordinary life"[23], and every subject should be understood by the students and teachers must teach clearly such subjects. Because, most of the students in the classroom were inelert and inactive to receive the communicated information by the teacher, here motivation is needed. While teaching, the teacher should try to motivate the children for their readiness. Thus, the students problems are interlinked with the inefficiency of the teachers, problem of understanding of the students and the subjects.

In Humanities and social studies subjects in the educational institutions, curriculum were given importance for the social awareness of the students. Values like honesty, promptness, discipline, courtesy, cooperation, diligence should be taught to the students for their good behaviour. The students should mould their character, cultivate virtue, maintain integrity and live for ideals.

All in all, these subjects present progressive knowledge and skills to the students. But from the moral point of view, the hidden values are to be cultivated and a climate of mutual understanding between students and teachers and mutual respect between them should lead students in their adult life.

Examinations System

Examinations are conducted by Educational Boards and Universities. The Dictionary meaning of the word examination is 'a test of capacity and knowledge'. The system of examination prevelent in our country in which a candidate answers to the questions which are containing in the blue-print. "One of the basic functions of an educational institution is to hold examination"[24] to eveluate the students knowledge and skills.

The 'Blue-print' contains the educational objectives, i. e., knowledge, comprehension, application, analysis, synthesis and evaluation. Thus, the examinations or tests are used to measure knowledge and understanding of the students. examinations are useful to the students to measure different kinds of purposes.

> The examinations are used for a variety of purposes for the grading of students, for promotion to the next class, as a diagnotic tool to discover areas of strength and weakness in the students, to judge the effectiveness of the teaching methods and to obtain a feedback, to select students for scholarship and talent; for placement of jobs, etc., and for subtly changing a curriculum for study in the event of development of new concepts[25].

The purpose of examinations clearly measures the students understanding, the knowledge which they acquired during the academic year. Examinations conducted by the concerned authorities in relation to the subjects "without receiving assistance for that purpose either from other or from text-books, extracts from text-books or notes or other paper brought to the examination hall"[26]. Thus, "the essence of the examination is that the worth of every person is appraised without any assistance from an outside source"[27].

Therefore examinations in educational institutions are held under strict discipline and the examination rules, i. e., "...that they must answer the questions without receiving any external aid or any aid other than their memory and the knowledge and proficiency acquired by them in the subject of undergoing the prescribed course of study"[28].

Written examinations in the modern period or in these days students are not yet met the aim of examinations but getting degrees with unfair means. Modern students are busy with the no-academic affairs which means they are involved with the political and other organisations and they neglect the regular studies. While writing examinations, students violate the rules and regulations and are commit malpractices of mass copying. There is student involvement with the mass copying. Thus, the:

> examinations assume proportions of a battle in which those responsible for conducting examinations face all kinds of threats, even to their lives if they try to stop or even interfere with the malpractices which are well organised between students and the outside anti-social elements and even the teachers[29].

It is common knowledge that written examinations these days are beset with numerous ills -use of unfair means by examinees and leakage of question papers to mention two important ones[30]. For example, it happened in the X class examinations of 1995 in Andhra Pradesh, the leakage of question papers regarding paperI Science and Paper-I and II of the Social Studies[31]. In this connection, according to Tiwari:

> In the way of public examinations are organized, the amount of time wasted in their organization and the corruptions

> involved in various operative parts at all levels- teachers, students, educational administrators, etc., should be enough to justify their abolition[32].

The system of examination in modern India has deteriorated, with all these disruptive background of the examinations and the real aim of examinations is being undone. The decline in academic standards are in a way related to the indisciplinary activities of the students. "The decline in academic standards is not unrelated to growing indiscipline among the students"[33], and decaying moral standards in the modern educational institutions. Arun Bhattacharjee defined:

> The mass copying in the examination is unfortunately becoming on unseemly feature of our educational institutions which is a reflection of the alarming decaying moral standards in all spheres of our country[34].

The causes for these problems among the students, if taken into consideration, reveals the deteriorated moral conditions of the students. In the modern conditions, students behaviour at the group and individual levels in the educational institutions and out of the institutions gives a clear picture of the situation. Causes for the indiscipline of misbehaviour in the students is related to the students personal and group attitudes and activities. Student's wrong attitudes towards morality is due to their parental up bringing, religious beliefs, financial position, social status, political leaders, unemployment, no future hope, etc. India suffered, in the past, on account of its scientific technological backwardness, but modern society is suffering with the deterioration of moral values.

The causes or reasons for the moral crisis or immoral behaviour of the modern students is due to lack of good manners.

> Students indiscipline is either simple bad manners or an invitable consequences of uncontrolled quantitative expansion, or an immitation of and exploitation by 'respectable' elders outside, mostly in political life[35] .

Employment Opportunities

Due to lack of employment opportunities, the modern youth at the higher levels of education are losing faith in true education and its degrees for they do not directly and immediately provide jobs. They join in higher education as there is no other way and stay there as long as they can. This situation made them lose their interest in the subject and the lessons and so abstain from attending the classes and aimlessly spend their time in the institutions. This brings frustration and frustration gives birth to anti-social and immoral actions. Large numbers, which are uncontrolable, join the institutions. The output is not planned in accordence with the demands of the community at the man power level, causing more unemployed youth. Youth are frustrated and are acting against the institution and its interests.

Causes for this are mainly contained in the influence of movies, the weakness of the administration, family conditions and political interference in education and lack of ideals of simplicity, honesty and "self-abnegation' in life, as well as, attraction towards material progress. In this context, K. L. Srimali defines:

> Past growing generation in India without a full awareness of its glorious heritage, the youngmen have little opportunity either in their homes or in educational institutions to become familiar with the great contribution which Indian civilization has made to art, literature, architecture, philosophy, and religion. Thus, their behaviour gives the impression in the way of material progress[36].

Thus, the problems considered in the students such as poor concentration, lack of interest in studies, also become causes for frustration. The mental or Pedagogic illness leads to the feeling of insecurity, feeling of complexity particularly an inferiority feeling, isolation and so on.

Financial Position

In India most of the students come from villages, and come to higher education, which is available in towns or cities. The students coming from villages get attracted towards the town culture, influenced by colleagues or peergroups. They spend much less time for studies and go out of the campus without any work.

Some of the students that waste their time are involved in anti-social activities. Some of the students belong to the rich or economically sound families, they waste time and spend more hours in a day, outside the campus. They has money to spend on unnecessary things like movies, and other disruptive behaviour like hard drinks and drug addition, etc.

The Parents' economic condition influences their children's behaviour. Poverty of the parents is one of the main causes of the students' frustration and indiscipline. Children of income, poor housing and unemployed "...may have severe consequences for the behaviour"[37] in educational institutions. Because they have poor housing conditions and inadequate facilities. Such students have generally poor concentration on studies due to lack of privacy to finish their homework and further reading. Students coming from these families, it is observed, are involved with group activities outside the institution. Lack of decision making and aimless or non-goal-oriented studies are the results. The disruptive students need the parents and elders control and supervision.

Student Union Elections

The College elections are also considered among the students indiscipline problems in the modern period, because the students are more concerned with the agitations through demonstration, strikes and violence in the campus and outside the campus in the name of college elections. In the modern times, college elections are causing problems and are also related to students unrest. Generally, students union elections in the educational institutions are introduced, in order importance to give basic training to period students in the way of democratic process in organising self-government. Thus, the students elections for the benefit of students to solve their common problems through their union. Students elections should not give to political and communal organisations interference, but in the modern students union elections are more concerned with the political leaders or parties and communal organisations interference. In this connection, "Increasing political influence in college union activities has led to violence, indiscipline and loss of human values. A way out is to hold union elections on non-party basis"[38].

> In early days of after independence, elections of school pupil leader, college union president, etc. based on secret ballots were introduced. During those days, disciplined and academically bright students were elected, and there was no outside interference. Activities too were held earnestly and with full cooperation of the rival groups[39].

The union elections created leadership crises among the students. Leadership crises are also named identitycrises later. In this regard, so many students participate in the union elections to contest in various panels.

Due to leadership crises, student groups in modern times are mostly influenced and controlled by the political parties and leaders as well as communal organisations. The outside organisations support various groups of the students, and the students are automatically divided into many groups as there are political parties, and it creates rivalry between them. Due to this, groupism and group rivalry, communal intolerance or caste feelings and regional feelings were developed. Sometimes some groups of students create more problems like instigating fighting between rival groups, and it leads to violence on the campus. These attitudes and misbehaviours of the students are considered as moral problems in the educational institutions in the modern period.

The political and communal interference in student elections cause more moral problems.

> This resulted in division and groupism among the students cooperation gave way to confrontation . To discredit each other or to show their strength, strikes were organised by rival groups. The students lost all finer feelings and respect for human values. This had its reflection in the entire society[40].

T. V. G. Nayer in his article mentions that, in schools and colleges by organisations having political affiliations, political leaders encouraged violence and indiscipline of the students indirectly. They see before them a handful of ministers of party big wigs who become successful in life because of their union activities in schools and colleges. They never see the hundreds of students who had lost their lives, health and their future because of the rivalries[41].

Even after elections are over, the modern student groups continue their rivalry and negative feelings. Yet, in various functions and celebrations held in the institution conducted by the elected union body, in this situation the rival groups try to distruct and conked out the programmes. "The organisers of such functions are also to blame, as rival groups are not taken into confidence"[42]. So, the students lost their tendency of cooperation "there is no give and take policy". Every incident and all activities are deepening with the rivalry. Political leaders and communal organisations are more connected with the student union elections in modern India and some of them "too add fuel to the fire when they get an opportunity".

The selection of the candidate to contest as a college union president is also made by the political party leaders and communal organisations. By the support of these outside wings, the student leader automatically elected but he has no academic talent and leadership qualities but has rowdy and goonda qualities.

This is also cause for the students' misbehaviour and disruptive behaviour in examinations. The student leader elected by the support of the external or outside wings would dominate the teachers and administrators of the institutions and he has to encourage the mass copying and other disturbances.

Most of the political leaders in our country had such type of experience while in their studentship. T. V. G. Nayer noted that:

> A Union Minister from Kerala had expressed his feeling of guilt for these kinds of activities which he had encouraged while he was a student leader. He had now advised students to desist from violence and solve their problems peacefully[43].

From the moral point of view, "more lipservice will not lead us anywhere but the moral rules and principles should be followed". Moral values and practice should be stressed in education to develop humane dealings in the institution and reduce the mal-practices and disorders in a system.

We live in the Atomic Age, but we forget that we also live in the Human Age. Instead of being armed with the atom, we should be armed with love, faith, joy and non-violence[44].

SECTION-II

Teacher's Misbehaviour: Some Causes and Remedies

> **The teacher need not, we can even say that he should not, try to draw out the underlying moral all the time; but if he has given some thought to the values underlying the scope of his subject and his work as a teacher, they will imperceptibly pass into his teaching and make an impact on the minds of his students.**

Report of the National Education Commission (1964-66), NCERT

Moral problems in educational institutions are not only related with the students but also with teachers. Teachers misbehaviour in the classroom, with regards to subject matter, and examinations and in the campus activities.

Human nature is a blend of both positive and negative attitudes and values. While children grow into adults, their negative values are subdued through education. In this context, teacher should manifest the positive attitudes and values among the children. Thus, teaching becomes an important aspect in the educational institutions.

Teaching is also concerned with the activities of the teacher and his or her attitudes towards the profession and students. The relation between the teacher and the students in the system of education assumes a valuable possession. The teacher, by his or her profession stands as a guide, promoter, friend and philosopher to his or her students. Teacher activities and attitudes therefore must be ideal, positive and progressive. "Being a teacher in India is not so much a single activity as it is pattern of coherent actions indicating awareness of one's place in the world"[45]. The teacher should have a thorough knowledge in his subject, "... the teacher must still learn his lessons, but he must also act, speak, live and value the things that will identify him as a teacher"[46].

Thus, teaching is an important element in the educational institutions. Teaching is an art and is a profession. "Teaching is not a science; it is a special kind of art, and it may be that only the artist can teach properly"[47].

According to A. S. Neill, that the teaching does not mean by the presentation of a lession; and it means "that the art of living with children" and "understanding them" and "being one of them"[48]. Thus the teacher could never ignore the students as well as the subject. The teacher has good identification in the society, and his or her reflections influence the society. In traditional India, very high place was given to the Gurus. In all respects, the modern teacher's position is deteriorating. Teachers also are involved in misbehaviour problems in modern Indian educational institutions. Their activities, which have deviated from the moral sphere, are not restricted to teaching, but are involving in other affairs also.

Class-Room Situation

The classroom is one of the key places in the system of education. The classroom has an unique identification for teaching-learning. The classroom is also a model of the integration and uniqueness. The teacher has a great role in the classroom.

Thus, the classroom is a centre for moulding and shaping of the student's personality through teaching. The teacher is one of the persons mainly responsible for the all-round development of the students. In the classroom, the teacher should behave gently and ideally before students and the teacher's behaviour and attitudes influence more on the students. Teaching as a programme, helps teachers mould students to meet their all-round development and the challenges of a changing society.

> The living classroom program helps teachers prepare students to meet the challenges of a changing world by having them resolve a variety of situations using rational problems solving. A sense of responsibility is fostered by helping students become involved in the educational process in that involvement leads to making choices for a person then feels responsible and to which he is communicated[49].

Thus the involvement of teacher-student in the classroom is essential for the system of formal educaton.

> This program also holds that concern for the individual is central. When teachers formulate objectives for students, they

> are demonstrating concern. Moreover, listening to the student listening to what he is really saying, and determining underlying needs will accelerate growth[50].

In the classroom, there are different kinds of students and their activities and attitudes also differ from each other. In this context, the indiscipline arises and the classroom gets disturbed. Therefore, the teacher has to control them and to do that he must be an authentic teacher. According to Tiwari, in our educational institution in modern times, students from different economic levels and different home conditions are receiving education. The deprived or disadvantaged children require a special kind of handling, a different kind of pedagogy[51]. But, in modern education institutions, the teachers are not following this direction. Tiwari finds out that, "it is unfortunate that nothing has been done in this direction and the teacher education institutions which have been stagnating as backwaters, have also failed to deliver the goods"[52].

In this regard the teacher has an important role while teaching in the classroom and managing the students especially unprivileged and disruptive children. Benerjee observes:

> the point for the moral teacher to bear in mind is, that he should watch the conduct of the pupil, ascertain where his weakness was that led to the slips, and try to guard against their repetition in future. If the errors are few and slight, they will in general be freely conferred, and the teacher will find it easy to correct them[53].

Therefore, the responsibilities of the teacher in educational institutions have to be studied. In the classroom, the teacher should clear doubts, and give direct answer to the students question. Teacher can give a chance to the students to express their own experiences and elaborate their ideas in a non-threatening manner. Thus, the teacher should have patience and control on the students.

But, modern teachers are not handling and managing the students in such a way. Teachers also have disciplinary problems. The teacher is to be respected by his students. Students are refusing the alienated teacher, that means, in modern times, some of the teachers are mishandling the students. If the teacher is authentic in a disciplinary situation, then the problem can be solved. In the case of alienated teachers or unfriendly teachers, they have to face the problems in the classroom. Address by Indira Gandhi:

> If the teacher is not himself or herself interested in the life and the world, he cannot be an interesting person, and therefore, his classes will be dull and if classes are dull, nobody learns anything[54].

There are many reasons or causes for the problems in the classroom. Teacher's behaviour and attitudes are the main causes of these problems, such as classroom control, motivation and maintaining himself as a model of ideal person, etc.

> A teacher in charge of control of a class has the undoubted right to maintain the discipline of the class and to regulate the conduct of the students in the class. So long as the students are in the class, they must deserve the rules of discipline, for otherwise there is bound to be a chaos or confusion in the class[55].

Generally teachers have many activities and duties regarding class-work. But,

> ... the present day teachers were paying much attention on out of class-work. Simultaneously they may not pay interest in teaching. They were not satisfied with the salaries not for the means of living but for the improvement of their social status. This leads to poor achievement of students[56].

This is considered a moral problem because the present day teachers are involving out of teaching or institutional activities. In fact, teachers should stay in the institution as per working hours in a day. It is also considered a classroom problem, because some teachers are not paying any attention to teaching in the classroom.

> Many people have spoken of the lack-luster teaching for examinations that takes place on the Indian campus, the crowded classes, the social distance between teacher and taught, and pernicious effect of rote learning[57].

Generally, in the classroom, teachers have disturbance from students many times. The classroom disturbance depends on many factors, such as inability and unmotivation of the students and disinterested and unskilled teachers, and it goes out of the teacher's control.

In this regard, "...teachers also recognised that there was typical students in classrooms"[58]. Teacher should find out the 'individual differences' among the students:

> Teacher 'typification' of pupils, identified, general care consideration; hard working or lazy type, mature or immature type, well behaved or poorly behaved type of the children[59].

In the higher educational institutions, the teachers are engaged in other activities than academic. The modern teachers especially at the higher levels are involving the student misconduct like groupism, casteism, and other feelings. Especially in the campus elections, teachers either directly or indirectly, give support to the student groups. In this connection teachers lose their respect from other groups of students, subsequently academic affairs are being neglected and the standards are coming down in educational institutions.

Another reason for teachers losing respect and leadership, lies in their acceptance of giving private tutions. The practice is so rampant that several state Governments have even banned it. There are some teachers who devote more time and attention to private tution than to their work in schools or colleges. The acceptance of money directly from the students has established a mercenary relationship, which has incapacitated the teacher from exercising authority or influence over the students' behaviour. There are few teachers who can virtues like honesty and integrity against the onslaught of opportunism and unprincipled manceures[60].

Subject Matter of Education

In modern educational institutions, teachers have problems along with individual and group activities, and classroom problems, problems with subjects, also have to be considered.

Teachers should have thoroughness in the subject matter and should follow methods in dealing with the instructional activities. The modern educational institutions are introducing modern branches of study which are more related with science and technology and management studies. In this regard, these disciplines are being stressed for the economic and technological development of the nation, but not in the social and moral aspects of development.

The discipline like History, Philosophy, Sociology Political Science, basically comprise the foundation study of education. Consequently, educational institutions are entertaining non-academic and business activities in modern India. Those studies are not trying to uplift their fields of knowledge scientifically, to make them more realistic and valid.

> In general, the theory of knowledge that is adhered to by those in the humanist tradition places less emphasis upon the scientific development of knowledge in the modern connotation of the word 'science' as necessarily involving careful experimentation, and more upon the securing of knowledge through the use of reason or the rational process[61].

Due to lack of proper knowledge on fundamental principles, values in education are being ignored. The materialistic thinking of the teachers and parents in the modern period gives importance to material development in education. Thus, the materialistic outlook is one of the causes of moral problems:

> As wealth and property is taken as a standard of sucess, parents teach the same to their children. Students read in books about the respect that is due to parents, elders and teachers and contrast it with the actual state of affairs[62].

In this regard students' tendency gets confused and leads to differences in theory and practice. They do not apply in their lives any importance to moral values and ideals:

> In such a situation, no moral education is bound to be successful. The atmosphere in present society is also not encouraging. Everyday one hears Scandals involving politicians, Ministers, Vice-Chancellors and such others. The fight for power and wealth has engulfed the nation in a web of corruption[63].

Regarding the students' misbehaviour in the institution, the teacher should control and act as a leader, without any bias. But modern teachers are another important reason for such behaviour, because students are losing respect towards them. Thus, the teacher has come to the level of thinking that delivering his lecture in the classroom is his only duty and that finishes his relation with the students. This is a circular action between students and teachers, he is losing interest in the students, because of the students' indiscipline, disinterestedness in the lessons, disrespect for him and thereby losing his interest in the subject and profession. But "while every professional is self-conscious about what he sets out to do, a teacher has of necessity to be much more self-conscious"[64].

This situation and student misbehaviour trend has put the teacher on guard by not allowing the students to have any close connection with him. In a situation where a student or group of them misbehave, he never interferes to stop that or advise them against doing such actions. In some cases, it happens that encouraging and using them for his own personal purposes, to take his own grudges on other teachers and administration. From the students' side, teacher-teacher, teacher-administration bad relations, on individual or group level have become bad examples for losing respect towards them.

Another reason for such behaviour is, backing of the different political parties and organisations to different groups of the community. The teachers from all stages of educational institutions and Universities were entertaining political parties and groups for the sake of their promotions and transfers in the case of school and college teachers. They are neglecting professional ethics and involve in corruption.

The cause of the problem is that the teachers are seeking social status and ambition for immediate benefits and promotions. For that benefit they are encouraging the students to indulge in misconduct and unusual activities in the campuses[65].

Scientific knowledge encourages materialistic development but it is not opposed to evaluating that knowledge, for the application to life for the common good. But the application of values to life is very difficult through the materialistic aspect.

Only good can come from the use of culture in our interpretation of social and moral development.

The teacher is an instrument, an agent, a guide to communicate the knowledge and skill to the students. Teacher should be well equipped and have mastery of the subject matter. Generally, teachers can adopt certain methods, to teach values and good attitudes to the students.

The Commission (1964-66) recommended that social, moral and spiritual values should be taught either directly or indirectly with the help of the ethical teachings of great religions.

It is true that the subject matter of such subjects should be taught by both direct and indirect methods of teaching, depending on the situation. The disciplines like History. Philosophy, Sociology and Politics have covered vast areas and have implied values and so these can be properly utilised to inculcate moral and spiritual values to the students.

Some of the institutions have faculty membere who are non-academic especially in private management institutions or autonomous institutions . Because they are appointing the teachers on the basis of nepotism and other politically influenced candidates. This type of appointed teachers is generally academically poor. In this connection, they do not take real interest in the subject matter, and do not follow academic methods of teaching. Moral education through other subjects - indirect method is also very effective at higher levels of education.

> This education, we believe should be provided, both by direct and indirect methods, by suggestion as well as by discussion and teaching. We attach great importance the role of indirect influence in building up good character. The school atmosphere, the faculties provided in the schools will have large say developing a sense of values[66].

Educational institutions would like to emphasize that the consciousness of values must permeate the programme of activities and the curriculum as a whole. In this regard, the teachers are not only in charge of moral instruction but they are responsible for character-building:

> Every teacher, whatever be the subject he teaches, must

> necessarily accept this responsibility. He must ensure that in the teaching of his particular subject and in his dealings with his pupils, fundamental values such as integrity and social responsibility are brought out[67].

The teacher helps the student to understand the subject matter and social realities. He or she should help the student to understand himself as a responsible individual in relation to society and to develop an awareness of his own potential. The Commission recommended that:

> The teacher need not, we can even say that he should not, try to draw out the underlying moral all the time; but if he has given some thought to the values underlying the scope of his subject and his work as a teacher, they will imperceptibly pass into his teaching and make an impact on the minds of his students[68].

Teacher should develop the 'social competence' among the students. He should motivate the students on the current events and should help them to the development of a creative mind. The teacher should emphasize the development of skills that enable the individual student to cope with problems of living, in a changing society.

Moreover, a sense of need and purpose should inspire all institutional activities and must be reflected in the life, sound and atmosphere of the institution. The assemblies, curricular and co-curricular activities, the celebration of festivals of all religions, work experience, games and sports, subject clubs, social service programmes -all these activities can help in inculcating the values of mutual cooperation and regard, honesty, integrity, discipline and individual and social responsibility. The modern educational institutions are not maintaining these values. These are an atavistic urge implement necessarily in every educational institution. "These values have a special importance in Indian society today, when young men and women are passing through a crisis of character"[69].

The indirect method of teaching is an 'internal activity', it is useful and sometimes an essential need to inculcate the values in education.

In this regard the teacher should have a sound grounding in

teaching the subject and attention to students in the classroom. The teacher should review himself and his contribution. It is also good to remember that:

> A poor teacher tells,
> An average teacher explains
> A good teacher demonstrates
> And a great teacher inspires[70].

From the point of teaching morals, the teacher should by his conduct inspire the students. While in the class room:

> If teaching is successful then some one must have learnt something, and to learn something is, in a very broad sense, to get some-thing right[71].

"Thus the success of the teacher depends on the success of the learner"[72] and vice-versa. In this connection, the methods of teaching depend on the subject matter and the curriculum as a whole. The Teacher should assist the student in utilizing available information or knowledge. He must encourage the students in the development of their intellectual ability, and skills to challenge the current social conventions to the development of social competencies.

In the direct method of teaching, the teacher helps the students attempt an experimental approach, by providing assistance and guidance only when needed. Teaching must emphasise the creation of collective and organisational skills and abilities that enable individuals to focus their unique personal competencies on the achievement of collective and ideal goals. In the direct method of instruction, we consider that the specific provision for moral instruction in the instutut ional programmes is highly desirable:

> At the secondary stage, there may be frequent discussions between the teacher and the pupils on the values sought to be inculcated. Whatever by the method of teaching, it should not lead to moral instruction being divorced from the rest of the curriculum or being confined to a single period. If the values are to be a part of the students character, on all-embracing treatment of the moral way of life is needed[73].

The higher educational institutions or Universities should

maintain the programmes of group discussions, conducting seminars and other programmes relating to the part of the development of academic skills as well as values in education.

Teachers should develop social and moral values. The teacher should help the students and motivate the social and ethical awareness among them. Ambiguity of the student's personal values and beliefs prevents the development of an integrated personality and confusion among social and moral values and beliefs, creates inter and intragroup conflicts. In this regard, the teacher must act deliberately to facilitate the person's development and clarification of individual and social values appropriate to the demands of the society.

In all respects, the teacher should help the student at any level of their studies to understand values and clarify the individuals' internal doubts and conflicts, on values. Most of the modern teachers are not ready to adopt such value patterned instruction method, because, they are busy with their personal and non-academic activities.

Examination System

In the examinations the teachers participate as invigilators as well as evaluators. The problem arises with teachers in the examination hall like encouraging the student's misbehaviour, such as the mass copying, attaching sheets, etc.; on the other hand, the teachers in evaluating the examination scripts are biased towards students based on caste, religion and regional, relatives and intimidators, etc.; and do not evaluate on the basis of genuine performance. There is no chance of student's misbehaviour unless teachers or invigilators help and encourage them. The political pressures and influences also play their role in influencing students.

All these situations lead to an immoral and non-academic environment of the institution as well as there is an imposition of the police force in the institution at the time of examinations. Consequently, the violent activities arise. That means the fighting between police and students. At last the total atmosphere gets spoiled by these situations.

Thus the teachers, students, administrators and the society

also should have an awareness of the system of examination. Students give importance to the passing of examinations without prior preparation and bothering about attendance and learning.

The pressures of number have altered the examination system. The manner in which schools and colleges admit students, the way teachers teach and the anticipated outcome of the process. "It is a system, very nearly out of control and one that promises of further deterioration unless a more comprehensive approach is fostered than has hitherto been evident"[74].

Examinations measure the students' knowledge and help the students to develop their memory power and to expressing their ideas and views on a particular subject. But, it is not fulfilling in the particular sense because the teachers and the authorities conducting the examinations do not strictly implement the rules and control the unruly behaviour of the students in the examination hall.

This situation should be controlled by the supervisors and the teachers should remind the students before examinations that they should not use any unfair means in the examination hall.

While examining the written examination papers are to be valued by the teachers who play as examiners, in this regard:

> Examiners played a part in evaluation; for that the essay-type questions, the marks reflect the mood and mental condition of the examiners. The same question examined by the same examiner under two different mental conditions may vary as much as 15% or even more, not to speak of two different examiners making the same set of papers[75].

In this aspect, the students who are the same and of equal standard were getting different marks in the examination.

Particularly from the point of view in examinations, teachers should help the students by properly teaching the subject matter and other values like honesty, discipline, etc., rather than help them to be dishonest.

Generally, examinations point out that the students strength and weakness, and it is a means to test the students' abilities. The system of examination plays an important role such as continuous assessment. Guided continuously by the teachers, these would help students to learn more techniques of 'problem solving', enhance their capacity for creativity in learning and thinking and help them to improve their knowledge and ability to communicate ideas in writing.

> The increasing incidence of mass copying, use of unfair means, the aggressive attitude of the youth, all this indicates that the purpose of examination has to be refined. For doing this, action is required, net reports. Perhaps to start with, we might do well to give a different name to the examination so as to change the connotation of the word. We should emphasise its pedagogic value rather than its demanding qualities. We shall make it a means to educate rather than an end in itself[76].

Thus the teacher should have social integrity and value-orientation awareness with the subject matter and content of the discipline. Therefore teacher and taught together with their efforts should a create moral atmosphere in the educational institutions.

SECTION-III

Administrators' Misbehaviour : Some Causes and Remedies

> Administration is the third leg of the trianlge, one is the student and another is the Faculty. Responsibilities on the administration are therefore more challenging today than before. The days of steel-frame organisation and rigid permanent rules are over.
>
> The Remarks of Dr. C. D. Deshmukh, Quoted from G. S. Gautam, *Crisis in the Temples of Learning*

Administrators are concerned with the students, teachers and non-teaching staff of the institution and with the Government and other academic governing bodies. Educational Administration, at the primary and secondary levels is under the control of 'Local Authorities', District Boards and State Boards.

State and Central Governments provide for the maintenance and establishment of educational institutions. SCERT and NCERT were also functioning at the State and national level for the development of education in our country. Higher education at the National level has been introduced under the control of both the State and Central Governments for the development of it. "The University Grants Commission Act of 1956, provides that the Commission was responsible for both the maintenance and development of Central and State Universities..."[77]

At all the levels of education, administration is in the hands of the heads of the institutions directly. The educational administrators are generally from the academic side to head the institution. The administrator has a responsibility of upholding academic standards and maintenance of the institution in a fitting way and maintaining good relationship with the government and public. Administrator, as a leader of the institution, should have 'moral complexity', if not the whole environment of the institution will have ill effects. "Administration is a moral act and administrator is a moral agent"[78].

Role of an Administrator

The word 'administrator' derived from the Latin word, administrate means to care for or to look after people, to manage affair[79]. Administrator in educational institution is to deal with the persons in the institution. The administrator should think abstractly of the persons to deal with many aspects. In this regard the administrator should have good qualities and positive attitudes like honesty, dignity, tolerance, power of decision making, sense of cooperation and dynamic leadership, etc.

> An 'organisation' is a combination of the necessary human beings, materials, toda, equipment, working space and appurtenance , brought to gather in systematic and effective correlations, to accomplish some desired object. Management is the force which leads, guides, and directs ... 'Governance' is the task of establishing rules and regulations and making of decisions that are required to regulate the activities of the organisation[80].

Moral and social skills, the administrator should utilise to determine the effectiveness of overall development of the institution and the students. The Principal or Heads of the institution have to play a key role in institutional administration and development. The quality of institutional administration depends on the quality of educational leadership and moral responsibility they provide. In this context, Ordway Tead defined:

> Administration is the comprehensive effort to direct, guide and integrate associated human striving which are focused towards some specific ends or aims...administration is conceived as the necessary activities of those individuals (executives) in an organisation who are changed with ordering, forwarding and facilitating the associated efforts of a group of individuals brought together to realise certain defined purposes[81].

In modern administrators like "Vice-Chancellor is ultimately responsible for everything that takes place at the University, all decisions are channeled through his desk"[82]. The University administration depends on the Vice -Chancellor's activities, attitudes and duties; some of them are :

To set objectives for using available resources;
To formulate plans for achieving these objectives;
To identify the activities to be performed;
To organise the activities into groups (departments);
To define the tasks to be done;
To group the tasks into jobs;
To staff the job with people;
To initiate work active ties;
To supply incentives to stimulate productivity;
To set up controls to measure the achievement of objectives;
To take remedial action if the objectives are not being met[83].

Administrator's Misbehaviour

Regarding modern educational administrators, many of them are not in reality good administrators, but they are administrators. Modern educational administrators are facing more problems from students and teachers when compared with other periods. The situation in primary and secondary educational institutions are not as problematic as in higher educational institutions.

Coming to the administrators at higher education, Principals and Vice-Chancellors are facing problems from the students such as indiscipline, strikes and gheraos and fighting for unjust causes, violence and other disturbances. The words of G. S. Goutam, in his book 'Crisis in the Temples of Learning':

> Outbreaks of students indiscipline and disorder have disruptive the academic life of Indian Universities on various occasions - strikes, demonstrations and gheraos of the Deans and the Vice-Chancellors and confrontation between the students on the one hand and the teachers and the community on the other are the events of daily news which we read every morning[84].

In reality administrators are the causes for such indisciplinary activities. These student problems arise in educational institutions sometimes due to bad relationship of the student-administrators. Most of the strikes, gheraos and violence take place in the colleges with the machinations of administrators. Some of the administrators with their selfish purposes are encouraging the students in such activities with the promises to protect them.

There are some misbehavioural problems from the administrators side also which have to be considered here. Modern administrators should be effective and leadership oriented.

> The administrators pretty well dominate the process. You want to talk about budgets -then yout better talk about faculty raises and money - then you better talk about administrators. You want to talk about expanding or cutting back on an academic department - You have to talk about administrators. You want to talk about relations to the outside or a new building or a special curriculum project - then you damn well better talk about administrators[85].

Causes for Problems

Administrators inability to control the campus disturbances leads to the dependence on police power and judicial actions; dishonesty on his part is leads to corruption; selfishness leads to the self support i. e., to stabilise the designation; non-democratic activities lead to Nepotism; casteism, etc. Likewise, these are the problems connected with the administrators in various levels of educational institutions, especially in higher educational institutions or universities.

But in the University, administrators support the students in many incidents, like all kinds of disturbances in the campus, because they have to protect their position and power in the campus, and this may lead to the imposition of the police force in the campus and legal support is needed for their activities. Legal actions are taken against them because of the opposition groups of the administrators. For example:

> Between the two extremes of absolute autocrat and democratic manager, the Vice-Chancellor vacillates in his own attitude towards job. When legal actions are instituted against him in the High court, as they frequently are, he is annoyed at the 'unruly' and indisciplined goondas (roughnecks) on the campus[86].

The modern youth in educational institutions dividing into groups, it leads to an identity crisis, because the administrators are giving more importance to the student leaders. Concerning admissions, the authorities should provide chances to the student leaders for admission into various courses irrespective of merit and so on. In this regard, the leadership crisis appears in the campus. "Youth today is frustrated and on the slightest protest these angry young men are ready to indulge in an orgy of violence"[87].

Most of the authorities are encouraging the student leaders to maintain their position and status, while appointments in various services in the campus, the administrators give preference to the 'Yes men circle' in various services.

The students who participate in the student elections and the elected student union members become nearer to the officials to participate in various occasions in the campus activities. The higher officials use the student's support to protect their personal and group interests.

"The increasing importance of the student union in the life of the average student is demonstrated by the emotional impact..."[88] In some cases, with the support of the student union, the administrator functions his duties and protects his position. He is biased towards his relatives, caste people, and 'yes men' circle, in various incidents like admissions, promotions, recruitment and so on.

Students cannot be blamed generally for misbehaviour, but some of the administrators are mainly responsible for such violences, the modern restlessness, stress, and conflicts among the students is only a reflection of the complete disorder and failures which exists in the modern educational institutions of India.

It is true that, in modern times, such misbehaviour of the administration is increasing. Thus "the Indian education system is becoming violent and, therefore, one is not sure how to analyse the phenomena"[89]. In this regard higher education in India should be provided good administration for moral strength to the all institutional groups, because, the problems are challenging modern administrators. Some of these problems are caused by administrators themselves directly and indirectly. Most of the institutions are always having minor problems or difficulties with the students and others who disobey rules and regulations. Similarly, administrators or authorities also violate the managerial rules and neglect ideal principles.

While concerning student elections, most of the higher officials are directly or indirectly supporting the student groups. Higher authorities and senior staff of the teaching faculty members are also maintaining student groups by the favouratism of caste, regional fractionalism. Evidently:

> In India, education has served as an instrument of caste or class survival. The Indian caste system itself is a unique social phenomenon which explains a number of educational ills. If one had no concept of India caste-autonomy or survival of people in terms of caste-Dharma, one would miss quite a bit of the finness Indian education attempts to exhibit[90].

It is not only wrong for the administrators, but with the system of Government and Government officers as well as political organisations who are delving into the disruptive activities. In this context:

> Some of you might retort that the situation in Universities is

> no worse than in the chambers of legislatures, where high standards or orderliness, discipline, and integrity are sadly lacking these days. It is unfortunately true that our generation has not been examplary in these respects and there is a growing coarseness, vulgority and apathy in our public life[91].

From the point of view of corruption it is a major problem in the present educational institutions. Mis-handling of the funds and corruption is mainly related to interference of the political leaders, sometimes the heads of institutions who did corruption without any pressures, which may indicate their selfishness. Corruption in educational institutions pertaining to the mishandling of the funds, selling spurious certificates or degrees and question papers were also at many times in the name of model papers, i. e., leakage of question papers.

Administrators had many responsibilities and power on institutional matters and things. Simultaneously, they have chances to disrupt the materials and mishandle the funds.

In modern campuses, mostly the administrative wing of the Universities are functioning in an unimaginative manner and they are the causes for the degeneration of the morality and academic quality. They are manipulate the rules for their own justifications. In this sense, they are dwelling in corruption. For example:

> Recently the citizen council of Meerut in a letter to the Chancellor allege]d that the appointments of many teachers and even professors in the Versity have been manuplated with the result that the Versity has "been stuffed with sub-standard Professors" in wilful violation of the provisions of the University act[92].

Thus the academic corruption and several things are manuplated with the influence of the Government and political leaders, as well as personal interest. Administrators are mostly appointing the Deans, coordinators and wardens who are a 'yes men' circle or followers of the authorities in many Universities. In this situation the responsibilities are decentralized but the powers of the Vice-Chancellor and the authorities are functioning positively in their own choice. "The University decision making bodies have been reduced to 'yes men'[93]".

The behaviour of the administrator is one of the important aspects of the educational administration. If the administrator's behaviour is morally good, then the institutional atmosphere can be good. The causes for these maladies are political interference, and the administrator's personal behaviour. Morality should be implicit in the personal and professional life:

> ... should administrators discuss their concepts of ethical behaviour, the discussion frequently involves such terms as trustworthiness, responsibility, loyality, honesty, legality, personal, productivity, and persistence[94].

Thus, the administrator's misbehaviour caused to their involvement in corruption. There are many sources of the corruption in the educational institutions or Universities. In this regard Amrik singh points:

> The two principal sources of corruption in our University life are, one, appointments, promotions and all that goes with it and, two, matters connected with the conduct of examinations[95].

Concerning appointments, the administrators, are manipulated to secure the influenced candidates. "This is another sphere where outside interference continuously undermines the authority of the University"[96]. These appointed teachers with recommendation from the sources of Government officials or any of the higher officials, political leaders and ministers, etc., they were lobbying inside and outside the campus and they do not take into consideration on academic affairs.

> For all the executive Government - and indeed for the political Government as a whole- the obligation to support integrity is greatest on the President and on his staff, who partake of influence. The obligation is greatest at that point because any deviation there multiplies itself in levels below. Lower levels are more vunerable and on them there is a moral obligation on behalf of responsible government to bend to presidential guidence[97].

Appointment committees, which are facing threats from the inside groups of the campus as well as outside of it. University authorities are fearful of the ruling party members, because, the Universities are dependent on Government for financial grants and support for the development and welfare of the University. The Syndicate or Executive Members of the University, are appointed by the Government. In this, the Government and the ruling party leaders directly entertain the University authorities. In return, the University authorities also entertain the Government and political party leaders.

The appointment of the Vice-Chancellors are made by the Government. In fact, some of the Vice-Chancellors are connected with the political parties. By the support, and interference of the political party leaders, the University authorities or Vice-Chancellors are involved with the corruption in the University administration. "The Vice-Chancellor today must be a mediater of diverse influence coming from the state and Central Governments as well as from the University itself"[98]. By such actions financial problems can be solved releasing more funds probably, but the immaterial moral problems in the campuses, no Government can solve, only institutional heads are responsible for that.

There are other causes for the failure of administration. In fact:

> The Indian education system is overloaded with too many objectives and every objective is considered equally important. It may not be surprising if one finds that the number of crises the system is facing is more or less the same as the numbeı of objectives with which the system is loaded, or the contradictions which are created by conflicting objectives[99].

Thus, the issues and contradictions which are faced by the modern educational administrators are, declining standards of academic consequences and irrelevance of educational affairs in the campuses. The fact is these problems are related to every member of the institution - it may be teacher, student or non-academic staff or administrator, and they have to play their vital roles within their responsibilities and they have to cooperate with one another for the welfare of the institution. In this regard, administrators should coordinate the members of the institution to share the responsibilities.

When the administrators neglect the responsibilities and rules and regulations, violent and aggressive incidents will be increased. The student indiscipline is caused by the loose administration without any control.

> The student felt that the Universities and colleges of present day are affected by the political activities. The political parties established their students wings in the Universities. These wings keep with their parent organisation. During the elections, agitations and demonstrations, these political youth wings play a dominent role. This whole process affects the University atmosphere as the students tend to be emotional and every incident is looked through particular angle[100].

Thus, conducting examinations is also a problem for the administrators, because, the students, particularly student leaders, have direct access to examination halls. Generally, many of the students are committed to mass-copying and some of the teachers are helping them because they have threats from student groups and they have a personal interest in helping their favourites and relatives. In the same way, the non-academic staff are also involve doing such things in every possible way. For example, arranging the Register numbers in the examination hall in the series, adding marks, etc., for their relatives, favourites, caste people and with the promise of a payment by the students, and so on.

> A variety of organised rackets run by unscrupulous elements, thrive on such a system of examination and some students turn to them as a last resort. Mass copying is encouraged by such a system leading to student in discipline and raising of purely diversonary slogans like the 'right' to 'cheat'[101].

The declining academic standards is caused to growing indiscipline of the students, although the cause for the latter are varied. The real source of this decline is the spread of corruption and lack of standards in the academic organisation itself. The situation has been deteriorating so fast that even the best known colleges and institutions have not escaped the decline in standards[102].

Another reason for the decline in standards in both academic and administrative context is the business oriented administrators in the Institutions and they may create the whole educational programmes for profit. "The whole system has become business proposition with the administration, the teachers and the students, all engages in deals by means of which degrees are bought and sold, question papers are traded and answer books are manipulated"[103].

The selection or appointments of the Deans and Coordinators as well as wardens are done on the basis of caste fractions and 'yes men' of the authorities on the hand, and on the other hand political influences are also entertained in place of merit and capacity.

> The whole University community, teachers, students and other staff is polarised on caste basis. The ideology of casteism animate, selection and promotion of teachers; admission of students, and other such policy matters.

The student pressure on the administrators, in policy matters is a common affair. Consequently, a large number of positions lie vacant for years together, because selections are delayed in view of the fear that if a person of one caste is appointed or promoted, the other caste people group would revolt. There have been numerous instances when Deans and Heads of the Departments initiated and played dirty politics, and organised violence. If a disciplinary action is initiated against the guild and the rival political groups pressure the authorities to withdraw the action or face the reper-cussions. There are very few appointments or promotions which materialize without the interference of civil courts[104].

Thus the crises in educational management are the administrator's personal attitudes and behaviour on one side and the other is mainly concerned with external political interference. "There are two main sources of external political interference which preclude the generation of corporate intellectual life. First, political parties misuse student leaders and teacher politicians to achieve their own political ends. Second, personal or political rivalries between persons in the government and those involved in University administration, often create conditions of crisis[105].

The cause for the moral problems among the administrators is due to lack of moral conduct and professional ethics in the functioning of the administration. "To fill the voids created by failure of an individual conscience to function in certain situations or by the inability to cover everything by a statute, codes of ethical behaviour for a profession were developed"[106].

Reasons for this: lack of cooperation between students and staff with administrators, selfish motives of the authorities and lack of self-respect etc., and the political interference.

> In fact, our political leadership today germinates in the University campus. Those a few who do not study and keep busy in creating problems in the campus, find significant position in future leader-ship. That is why corruption and immorality are inherent characteristics of our political leadership these days. The undesirable elements who are planted and nourished by the political parties inside the campus are later on inducted into national politics. They are trained in creating problems, and politicising minor issues for the benefit of political ends at the cost of corporate academic life in the Universities[107].

Some Remedial Measures

In modern administrators, like "Vice-Chancellor, is ultimately responsible for everything that takes place at the University, all decisions are channeled through his desk"[108].

> The virtual collapse of the education system in our country is a patent fact, so much so that most of us have lost interest in discussing possible remedies. The all too frequent violence on one campus or another makes sure that the issue remains in the head lines almost all the time. But we all treat it as a routine occurances. It no longer shocks us; it no longer provokes us to think what can be done to improve things. Perhaps without knowing it, certainly without saying it we have convinced ourselves that the problem is hopeless, that there is little anyone can do about it[109].

Generally the University administration should maintain values which are being neglected in the modern administrators as:

> The administration and academic wings of the University must work in a spirit of cooperation, understanding and imagination, and the human touch must be present on the University campus, in the classrooms, co-curricular activities and even in

> purely administrative matters. Lines of communication between different sections of the University community must always remain alive and should never be allowed to be blocked[110].

Therefore, the administrators should have an awareness of the social and moral values for the maintenance of the peaceful atmosphere in the campuses. In this context, Kumudben Joshi suggests:

> If you want peace in the campus of any University and if we want happiness amongst the parent-student community alike, it is for elder generation and social leadership to create the proper environment for such peace and good will amongst all sections of our students. Unless we create that good will and love with in the campus of every educational institution and unless we produce that atmosphere of peace, we have no right to expect if of the student and the youth groups[111].

Administrator should try to achieve the aims and objectives of the institution. Universities are established for the development of academic excellence and to fulfill the aims and objectives of the higher education. In the words of Jawaharlal Nehru:

> A University stands for humanism, for tolerance, for reason, for the adventure of ideas and for the onward march of the human race towards even higher objectives. If the Universities discharge their duties adequately, then it is well with the nation and the people[112].

To achieve the aims and objectives of the educational institutions - administrators should always maintain the reality of the activities such as, 'authority' and 'responsibility', control or good direction, secure the good will of personal, public educational departments and other social agencies relationship and coordination in functions[113]. Coordination is an essential element of the functions of an administrator which is mishappening no modern times, thus lack of coordination may result in weakening administration.

Therefore, administrators should have wider understanding on administration, otherwise the environment of the institution could be polluted. "Educational Administration is to enable the right pupils to receive the right education from the right teachers, at a cost within the means of the state under conditions which will enable the pupils best to profit by their training[114].

Thus the administration is also concerned with the administrator's behaviour and activities. In this context, the administrator should be elert, particularly in the point of view on pedagogic matters and should have self-control. Co-existence is an essential quality of administration. Where "Co-existence", means tolerance of the individuals between one group and another group. It is the part of integrity between groups. There are so many groups in the University, such as, student groups, teacher groups, and other working staff of the University. These groups may cause problems to the administrators. Therefore, there must be co-existence and that is the best policy to make a peaceful environment in the campus.

> If we, therefore, wish to adopt a philosophy of active co-existence, our fundamental attitude that we are the professors of light and others are grovelling in darkness will have to be abandoned[115].

Educational Administration, should have both a theoretical and a practical approach and it should be adopted by the administrators. That theory and practice must emphasize the integrity and purpose of the institutional persons and groups as a whole.

The administrators of educational institution, should maintain the moral qualities. They can be classified as below. They are:

> Ability to discriminate right and wrong Belief in Democratic values. Ethical values, Good character, highest ideals, Ready to admit mistakes, self-control. Self-realisation through social service. Self-respect and sense of absolute values[116].

The administrator should be able to control the groups of the institution. Every group in the campuses have strength with unions such as, Teacher's Union, Non-Teaching Staff union and students' Union. The administrator should have the moral courage to coordinate and have control over the groups.

References

1. R.N. Vyas, *Education at the Cross Roads*, p. 66.
2. R.N. Vyas, *Op.cit.*, p. 67.
3. Gandhi, *True Education (The Servants of India Society)*. p. 46.
4. *Idem.*
5. *The Curriculum for the Ten-year School - A Framework* (NCERT), p. 5.
6. S.P. Pani and R. N. Pani, *Journal of Indian Education*, May, 1985, p. 64.
7. U.S. Madhyasta, *Journal of Indian Education*, May, 1978, p. 34.
8. R. L. Nigma. *Youth in Frement, edited by R. C. Gupta*, P. 43.
9. Arun Bhattacharjee, *Misconduct of students - A Legal and Disciplinary Study*, p. 15.
10. S. L. Makkar, School Discipline. *Journal of Indian Education, May*, 1988, p. 42.
11. *Idem.*
12. A. Kraft, *The Living Classroom Putting Humanistic Education into Practice*, p. 133.
13. A. Kraft, *Op. cit.*, p. 133.
14. A. Bhattacharjee, *Op. cit.*, p. 34.
15. A. Kraft, The Classroom, *Op. cit.*, p. 170.
16. *Idem.*
17. *Ibid*, pp. 133-134.
18. D. D. Tiwari, *Education at cross Roads*, p. 39.
19. John Wilson, Norman Wilson and Barry Sugarman, *Introduction to Moral Education*, p. 142.
20. Arthur Kraft, *The Living Classroom*, p. 239.
21. C. L. Sapra and Y. Aggarwal, *Education in India*, p. 25.
22. S. P. Pani, R. N. Pani, *'A New Outlook on Education', Journal of Indian Education*, May 1985, p. 65.
23. K S. Murty. *Ethics, Education, Indian Unity and Culture*, p. 35.
24. Arun Bhattacharjee, *Misconduct of Students*, p. 20.
25. K. K. Rohatgi and Mukherjee, *Profiles of Indian Education*, p. 113.

26. Bhattacharjee, *Misconduct of Students*, p. 21.
27. *Ibid*, p. 20.
28. *Ibid*, p. 21.
29. J. D. Sethi, *The Crisis and Collapse of Higher Education in India*, p. 3.
30. N. K. Suryanarayana, *The Hindu*, Tuesday, March 14, 1995.
31. *The Hindu*, 3rd April, 1995.
32. D. D. Tiwari, *Education at the Cross Roads*, p. 39.
33. J. D. Sethi, *Op. cit.*, p. 61.
34. A. Bhattacharjee, *Op. cit.*, p. 9.
35. R. L. Nigma, *Youth in Fremat*, edited by R. C. Gupta, p. 43.
36. K. L. Srimali, *A Search for Values in Indian Education*, p. 31.
37. Motimer and Davies, *Behaviour Problems in Schools*, p. 9.
38. T. V. G. Nayar, *The Hindu, Education Column*, Tuesday, 17th December, 1991.
39. *Idem.*
40. T. V. G. Nayar, *Op, cit.*
41. T. V. G. Nayar, *Op, cit.*
42. T. V. G. Nayar, *Op, cit.*
43. T. V. G. Nayar, *Op, cit.*
44. R. P. Bhatnagar and Aggarwal, V, *Educational Administration*, p. 19.
45. J. Bona, *Critical Perspectives on Indian Education*, p. 179.
46. Idem.
47. L. R. Perry, *Educational Thinkers Series*, p. 161.
48. *Idem.*
49. A. Kraft, *The Living Classroom*, p. 17.
50. Idem.
51. D. D. Tiwari, *Education at the Cross Roads*, p. 39.
52. *Idem.*

53. G. D. Benerjee, *A Few Thoughts on Education,* p. 148.
54. *All India Conference of District Education Offices,* New Delhi, March 6-8, 1978, p. 290.
55. Arun Bhattacharjee, *Misconduct of Students,* p. 30
56. K. Sudhakar Rao, *Educational Review,* Jan. 1995, p. 2.
57. Joseph Di Bona, *Critical Perspectives on Indian Education,* p. 179.
58. Ivan Read, *The Sociology of School and Education,* p. 102.
59. *Idem.*
60. Y. G. Muralidharan, *The Hindu,* Sept. 3rd, 1991, "Education Column".
61. Hurwitz Emmanuel, Jr. & Charles A. Tesconi, Jr. , *Challenges to Education Readings for Analysis of Major issues,* p. 11.
62. Y. G. Muralidharan, *The Hindu,* Sept. 3rd, 1991.
63. Y. G. Muralidharan, *The Hindu Daily News Paper,* Sept. 3rd, 1991.
64. Amrik Singh, *Redeeming Higher Education, Essay in Educational Policy,* p. 173.
65. The Statement concerned with some of the teachers who are involved in those incidents but not all of the Teachers.
66. *Report of the National Education (1964-66), NCERT,* p 359.
67. *Ibid.,* p. 358.
68. *Report of the National Education (1964-66), NCERT,* p.358.
69. Report of the National Education Commission, *Op. cit.,* p. 359.
70. J. C. Aggarwal and S. P. Aggarwal, *Educational Planning in India,* p. 185.
71. Glen Lagford, *Education, Persons and Society: A Philosophical Enquiry,* p. 126.
72. *Idem.*
73. Report of the National Education Commission (1964-66), *Op. cit.,* p. 359.

74. Joseph DiBona, *Critical Perspectives on Indian Education*, p. 10.
75. K. K. Rohatji-Mukherjee, *Profiles on Indian Education*, p. 112.
76. K. K. Rohatji-Mukherjee, *Profiles on Indian Education*, the Golden Jubilee Celebrations Committee of the Parle Tilak Vidyalaya - Collection of Essays on Indian Education, 1771, p. 111.
77. K. L. Shrimali, *The Myth of University Autonomy and Other Essays*, p. 12.
78. Ordway Tead, Administration: *Its Purpose and Performance*, quoted om Prakash Sharma, Administration of Education Boards in India, p. 72.
79. *Idem*.
80. William J. Schulze, *Administration*, Oxford and IBH Publishing Co. , New Delhi, 1970, p. 36.
81. Ordway Tead, *The Art of Administration*, pp. 3-4.
82. Pradeep, R, Mahendiratta. *Op. cit.*, p. 42.
83. G. S. Goutam, *Crisis in the Temples of Learning*, p. 94.
84. Baldidge, Victor and Associates, *Policy making and effective leadership*, Jossy-Bass Publishers, San Fransisco, 1978, p. 74.
85. Di Bona, Joseph, *Op. cit.*, p. 178.
86. K. L. Shrimali, *A Search for Values in Indian Education*, p. 91.
87. Di Bona, Joseph, *Op. cit.*, p. 207.
88. J. D. Sethi, *The Crisis and Collapse of Higher Education in India*, p. xiii.
89. Di Bona, Joseph, *Op. cit.*, p. 2.
90. K. L. Shrimali, *Op. cit.*, pp. 36-37.
91. J. D. Sethi, *Op. cit.*, p. 8
92. *Ibid*, p. 9.
93. B. D. Bhatt and S. R. Sharma, *Educational Administration*, p. 182.
94. Amrik Singh, *Redeeming Higher Education, Essays in Educational Policy*, p. 134.
95. K. L. Shrimali, *Op. cit.*, p. 66.

96. B. D. Bhatt and S. R. Sharma, *Educational Administration*, p. 183.
97. Di Bona, Joseph, *Op. cit.*, p. 176.
98. J. D. Sethi, *Op. cit.*, p. 21.
99. K. Srinivasa Rao, *University Discipline and Law: A Socio-Legal Analysis*, Osmania University Publication, Hyderabad, 1978, p. 23.
100. A. S. Ramakrishna, *'Examination Reforms', Journal of Indian Education*, July 1988, p. 19.
101. J. D. Sethi, *Op. cit.*, pp. 61-62.
102. C. P. Chauhan, *Op. cit.*, p. 153.
103. S. P. S. Chauhan, *Op. cit.*, p. 158.
104. S. P. S. Chauhan, *Op. cit.*, p. 162.
105. Quoted B. D. Bhatt and S. R. Sharma, *Op. cit.*, p. 187.
106. C. P. S. Chauhan, *Op. cit.*, p. 163.
107. Di Bona, Joseph, *Op. cit.*, p.177.
108. *Times of India* - Editorial on 17th October, 1982.
109. Pradeep, R. Mahendiratta, *Op. cit.*, p. 53.
110. Kumudben Joshi, Treasury of Living words. *A selection from the speeches of a Governor*, p. 27 (extension lecture at the Goa University on 2nd June, 1988).
111. Suresh Bhatnagar, *Kothari Commission (Recommendations and Evaluation) Loyal Book Depot*, Meerut, 1972, p. 95.
112. R. P. Bhatnagar and Agarwal Vidya, *Educational Administration (Planning and Supervisions)*, Anupama Publishers, Delhi, 1986, p. 42.
113. Graham Balfour's in his book *'Educational Administrations'*, quoted R. P. Bhatnagar and Aggarwal, Vidya, Educational Administration, p. 13.38.
114. S. Radhakrishnan, *Occasional Speeches and Writings*, p. 53. (Address at the Commissioner's Reception at the Indian Sports Club, 7th July, 1956).
115. R. P. Bhatnagar and Vidya Aggarwal, *Op. cit.*, p. 187.

6

Conclusions

... There is a great deal of talk of corruption and dishonesty in our official and business life. It is the students of today who are to be in-charge of the various departments of life tomorrow, and if they learn what real integrity is in their early years, there are not likely to go very far wrong later on. Every effort must, therefore, be made to teach students true moral values from the earliest stage of their educational life ...If the content of education is also enriched with moral and spiritual values, the purpose of education will have been truely fulfilled.

The Committee on Religious and Moral Instruction, Government of India, 1959

India in the traditional period has to face many problems and to struggle for its survival. First the invasion of Aryans, a more advanced race than the Dravidians, the original settlers. Dominating the natives they occupied India mainly the Northern parts, and permanently settled. They made an advancement in knowledge, possessing their own culture, spread it in India and finally that culture received the honour of being named as the Indian culture, mainly of course, there was naturally a mixture of southern culture also. Aryan India advanced notably in many fields like religion, philosophy, science, art, architecture, social and political organisations, etc. Among the Aryan race, Brahmins, the priestly class, were especially responsible for the advancement of knowledge and therefore, they took up the profession of teaching, to hand over the existing knowledge, customs, habits etc., in the name of tradition to the younger generations, to train them as fitting members of the community and to preserve the cultural heritage. And above all these purposes of education, there was the fundamental aim of making the youth realize themselves, i.e., what is the purpose of their existence in the world, and their relation to the creator, and the ultimate reality of the eternal life, and what potentialities and capacities they possess and how to realise and put to better use for the welfare of humanity. Actually, imparting of such knowledge, helped the youth to develop into real human beings. In the basic aims of education there was no distinction between religious and moral values and ideals, they both were one and the same. Therefore, education imparted knowledge and training in the religiously moral way of life, to attain fulfilment in life here and to attain Mukti after this life.

Depending on the main end of education, the content of it was selected to attain that aim, that of, religious scriptures like the Vedas, Brahmanas, Upanishads, etc., and the methods were to train them in theoretical as well as in practical knowledge. Practical classes were held at the places of temples and religious occasions and festivals in the houses in performing 'puja' or worship of different Gods. And for attaining the highest knowledge and Mukti, meditation methods were taught. The students were accepted from the three upper castes only, showing a distinction among the people. Brahmin priests, mainly were the teachers and there existed a very cordial relationship between the teacher and the taught, like father and son.

The situation of accepting the religious basis of morality was so until the advent of secualr morality in the modern period. But such a division in some ways negatively affected modern behaviour patterns of the youth, in not having the fear or desire of achieving moral and religious ends in this and the after life. The Nation and the people and along with them their educational aims, turned to be mostly materialistic and this situation brought in the modern youth, in general, carelessness about anything that affects either religious or moral values and behaviour. To make a strong criticism on modern education is that, it is almost totally failing itself from such basic ideal in life and thereby, doing, knowingly or unknowing, a dangerous set back in the path of survival and advancement of the human race. If humanness is not helped to develop in the younger generation, they act inhumanly and anti-humanly and thereby destroy themselves and ultimately the human race itself.

Traditional India, in the 6th Century B.C. witnessed the upsurage of Buddhism as a revolt against Hinduism, and especially the priest class. But it could not totally reject it, as both were from the same soli and cultural tradition. Rhys Davide points that, actually Buddha was considered by the Hindus as "... the greatest and wisest and best of the Hindus". This was a modification of Hinduism and had its base deep in Hindu philosophical thought. It brought tremendous changes in the social and cultural outlook of the poeple. It abolished the Hindu caste distinctions and brought equality of all people. Buddhism worked for religious rejuvination, and stressed the importance of following its moral values and principles in fulfilling individual and social life of its adherents.

Buddhism founded its own educational practices and was a revolt against the Vedic education, but resembled it in many aspects. Education was scattered to the religious and secular needs of the people. Unlike Hindu education, Buddhist education allowed everybody to enter into their institutions without any restrictions. Monasteries were the main places where education was imparted. Individual emancipation was the fundamental aim of Buddhist education. Buddhist education was of two types, one for those who completely reject this worldly life and strive for their spiritual development, as monks, and the other type is for the house-holders, who through their worldly life, work for their salvation. For the first, pure spiritual education was imparted, for the other secular subjects combined with spiritual education was given. Secular education was added to the original spiritual education to enable others also to adopt Buddhism. Moral values and practices assumed the main basis for their spiritual growth. It aims, content of education, methods of teaching, discipline and most of it, was adopted from the Vedic education. Students were put to rigorous moral discipline, especially those who were destined to become monks. The whole educational atmosphere was spiritual and moral. Teachers were made for their high standards of moral life. Strict disciplinary actions were taken against the miscreants according to the set rules. Developing the moral dimension of the youth led to the spiritual growth and attainment of Nirvana or emancipation, from the vicious circle of births and deaths.

Medieval India, had to face terrible setbacks in its cultural advancement and peaceful life ways, by the invasions of "Moslems". These people, not only robbed the country of its wealth by their raids, but also destroyed its important places of worship and learning and made it helpless and more weak and to struggle hard for its survival and identity itself. After the military raids captured some of the important places and established their rule in India and permanently settled. To make their numbers more and to spread their religion, they either by pursuance or compulsion made Indians convert to Islam.With this step, they then constructed Mosques for worship and the Quran as the basis of Islam had the sole authority, to conduct them in any walk of their life, either political, economical, social or moral. The Mosque in Moslems culture occupies a very important place and these were used not only for worship, but as seats of learning. Education assumed a specifically important position in the lives of the youth, because, if they were to develop into true Muslims, their life must be based on Islamic principles, and for that they must be taught thoroughly the Quran. As in traditional India, the Vedas occupied the main content of its education , the Quran was given the same prominence. Muslim culture was totally dominated by their religion, so was their education and there was no distinction between religious morality and social morality, they were one and the same. This reveals that, their education was mainly meant to develop the moral behaviour, or character of their youth, to make them fitting members of their Islamic society and to spread its values to others. This fundamental purpose of education, provided their youth, an opportunity to know themselves, and to lead more meaningful and fruitful religiously moral lives. This type of moral bent of mind and behaviour is not witnessed in modern Indian youth.

India entering into the modern period, had to struggle hard to survive. Somehow it could withstand Muslim invasions and comprimise with their settlement in some parts and taking hold of political dominence and spread of their own religion along with their culture at the cost of Indian traditional culture. Britishers entered India and completely made it a colonial country and established their own western models in all the fields of human activity. Western culture with its religion, Christianity, brought changes in the oriental culture. As Muslims were insterested strongly in spreading their religion, the Britishers were also of the same intension made conversions. To spread their religion and to establish their rule permanently, they resorted to take hold of the education of the people. They started their own type of educational institutions at all the levels, and to bring modifications in oriental education to suit their aspirations and needs. The British model of education was originally based mainly on spiritual and moral values of Christianity. But British rulers themselves never really followed the fundamental principles of the Christian religion, which is full of moral commandments and exhortations to lead a sacrificial life, if not, they would not occupied India, another peoples property, and established their own rule and robbed India of its precious wealth, and treated them as slaves inhumanly in their own land. They must be the people who crucified Jesus Christ again, of course spiritually. If Christ were an Indian at that time, and preached against their worldly lusts and ambitions, certainly they would have crucified him, physically also. Britishers could not withstand themselves before the moral strength of Indians, which they were lacking, and left India to itself ultimately and leaving their (not their selfish type of religion). Christianity, the real one, to survive in the hearts of true believers of India. But they neglected to aim sincerely for the development of the moral and spiritual aspects, in adopting the British model on Indian soil. What they wanted was middle men to communicate with the people and help in controlling them. Their educational interests were largely restricted to training the youth for subordinate positions in their Government. For that, they had to introduce English, the communicating language, as a medium of instruction, and to introduce modern subjects like science and technology to develop the country economically for their economic benefits.

In the true sense of education, the economic benefits was not imparted, and lacked human touch and morality, and with a differential context it was extended to Indian youth, that is mainly to make them obedient and subordinate to them and accept those superiority and authority. When compared to the fundamental aim of education of helping the youth to lead a pure moral life and to make his individual and social life, meaningful and worthy to live.

Education in post-Independence India, felt relieved of its iron shutters of the British rule and aimed to sour high in freedom to revive its own cultural tradition. But to the contrary, it was realized that, after coming in touch with the Western economic, political and educational systems, and knowledge of, especially advanced sciences and technologies, which possess mainly utilitarian purposes, it could not deny the western dominence in reality. If India had to protect itself from any more foreign invasions in the future, it realized that, it had to strengthen itself in political and economical fields, and military forces and modernize along with other countries and develop industrially, using modern science and technology and for that it had to adopt western models in its educational system. But Indian education could not directly and totally import the western type, because of the cultural differences. Therefore, the Indian Government appointed committees and commissions on different aspects and levels of education, to find out smooth ways of not undermining the traditional Indian heritage to be transmitted to the younger generation for its continuation, but at the same time, making better use of the western knowledge, by introducing in the curriculum western science and technology to develop the country on modern lines.

Indian education from the beginning is noted for its moral and spiritual aims, working as a foundation and all pervading influence. Coming to the medieval Muslim cultural invasion and influence to some extent it deviated from its original purity of aims. And next, the western impact destroyed it to a large extent. Of course, some oriental orthodox Hindu educational institutions tried to preserve its culture and aims, but nation wide could not do that. No doubt, modern scientific knowledge has become a blessing to India. But modern education, in its haste to adopt to progressive western ways, undermined the fundamental purpose of helping to lead the youth on moral and spiritual path, thereby facing unimagined crises in the educational institutions especially higher education and it is going beyond its portals and effecting the social life of the citizens. The repercussion are pointing a danger mark to take immediate steps. Indian Government is well aware of the dangerous situation and therefore introduced in educational aims, religious and moral values, to help to build the character of the youth, on the strong recommendations of the educational commissions appointed to study the situation.

But the sorry state of things is, all the aims and objectives, which stress the moral aspects of the youth, are on paper only. Because though they could mark the ways and means of adopting them, those who are directly concerned in implementing them are not in a position to do that and it has many reasons. The Government , i. e., the ruling political party itself is in some ways responsible for the youth misbehaviour to serve its selfish ends. Starting from them in the ladder of heirarchy, at every level, those involved in the educational endeavours are not committed to serve these aims, in their personal and social life because they are corrupted themselves, for their personal benefits. Administrators and teachers are the persons who themselves misbehave and mishandle the students and turn them into anti-social and immoral and send them into the world to make their life and others in the society wreched and miserable, deviating utterly from the grand and honourable aim of making individual and social life, more meaningful and worth living.

Many remedial measures have been already prescribed in the Government Committees and commissions and policies, but the thing is, who are involved in this great work of 'bring up' the youth of the society are to clean their conscience first and rededicate themselves with a new zeal to serve the country and the humanity.

In modern Indian education implementing the spiritual and moral aims are in the hands of different sections of people who are involved in the joint venture of educating the youth. Whereas in the traditional period, those aims were set and the teacher was the sole authority in educating the youth and he used to take much pains to develop the moral behaviour of the students by closely observing them at every point. Of course, this was because students were fewer in number, and living with him in close relation as a father and son. And nobody was there to question his authority, as even the rulers had to take the advise of the teachers in ruling their kingdom. In reality, a teacher was also a Raja Guru, used to assume the highest honour in the kingdom, and even the king had to respect and accept his superiority.

Suggestions

Contemporary system of education should be remoulded on the foundations of the traditional moral values and practices, in the light of the present day experiences and scientific knowledge.

The subject-matter of education must be linked with the life experiences and needs and aspirations of the people. The curriculum must be reconstructed in those lines and should be comprehensive and education and school must linked with productivity and community, respectively.

Education must impart knowledge of the moral code and conduct and must provide practical guidance and models. A final moral sense must be aroused in the youth like brotherhood, sympathy, love, cooperation, charity, helpfulness, forgiveness, etc. Individual differences of the youth should be taken into consideration while guiding them. The examination system must be changed with better means to value the worth of the students, instead of the present type of valuing the cramings of the students. There should be developed methods to test his moral behaviour. Work-experiences, and social work must be made compulsory at all levels of education, so that, children would develop a sense of responsibility and belongingness, and also develop service mindedness and not selfishness. These will help them to be morally conducted in their individual and social life.

Education must be redefined to meet the moral challenges in a better way in its institutions. Teachers must be made to realise their responsibility of moulding the character of their students, by being models themselves. The personal lives of the teachers must be taken into consideration while appointing them and also regular checks must be there by the concerned authorities, because unruly teachers produce unruly students. Administrators must be highly academic and morally praiseworthy persons to serve the aims of the Institutions in a sincere and dedicated manner. Administrators and teachers are the key persons in influencing the behaviour of their students, with their personal and social life and therefore they must help to produce a moral atmosphere in the educational institutions in order to develop the morality of the students.

Bibliography

Achyuthan, Mavelikara : *Educational Practices in Manu, Panini and Kautilya,* Jayajotsna, Jawahar Nagar, Trivandrum.

Aggarwal, J.C. : *The Progress of Education in Free India,* Arya Book Depot, New Delhi, 1966.

Aggarwal, J.C. and Aggarwal, S.P. : *Educational Planning in India, with a slant to Educational Financing and Administration,* Concept Pub. Co., New Delhi, 1992.

Aggarwal, J.C. : *Development and Planning of Modern Education with special reference to India,* Vikas Publishing House Pvt. Ltd., New Delhi, 1982.

Aggarwal, J.C. and Bhatt, B.D. : *Educational Documents in India (1813-1968)* (Survey of Indian Education) Arya Book Depot, New Delhi 1969.

Altekar, A.S. : *Education in Ancient India,* Nanda Kishore & Bros., Varanasi, 1965.

Archie J. Bahm : *Ethics the Science of Oughtness,* Abbreviated Edition, Archie J. Bahm Publishers, Albuquerque, New Mexico, U.S.A. 1984.

Benerjee, G.D. : *A Few Thoughts on Education,* S.K. Lahiri & Co. Cotton Press, Jotish Chandra Ghosh, Calcutta, 1910.

Benton, A.H. : *Indian Moral Instruction and Caste Problems,* Classical Publications, New Delhi, 1978.

Bhattacharjee, Arun : *Misconduct of Students : A Legal and Disciplinary Study,* Deep and Deep Publications, New Delhi, 1981.

Bhatt, B.D. and Sharma, S.R. : *Educational Administration, Emerging Trends*, Kanishka Publishing House, Delhi, 1992.

Bhatnagar, Suresh : *Kothari Commission, Recommendation and Evaluation, with a Text on National Policy on Education*, Loyal Book Depot, Meerut, 1972.

Brubacher John S. : *Modern Philosophies of Education*, Tata McGraw- Hill Publishing Co. Ltd., New Delhi, 1983.

Butts, R. Freeman : *A Cultural History of Education, Reassesing our Educational Traditions*, Mc-Graw Hill Book Company, INC, New York, 1947.

Bull Norman I. : *Moral Education*, Routledge & Kegan Paul C. Tinling & Co. Ltd., London, 1964.

Castle, E.B. : *Moral Education in Christian Times*, George Allen and Unwin Ltd., London, 1958.

Chkravarti, Atulanand : *Thoughts on Indian Education*, Ministry of Education and Scientific Research, Govt. of India, 1958.

Chapman, J. Crosby : *Principles of Education*, H. Mifflin, New York, 1924.

Chatterjee, C. : *Vedantic Education*. Gaurange Cultural Research Institute, Lucknow, 1957.

Chatterjee, Kalyan, K. : *English Education in India, Issues and Opinions*, The Macmillan Company of India Limited, Delhi, 1976.

Chaube, S. P. : *History of Indian Education*, Vinod Pustak Mandir, Agra, 1988.

-- : *A Survey of Educational Problems and Experiments in India*, Kitab Mahal Private Ltd., Allahabad, 1965.

Chaudary, Harish Chandra : *Management Education in India*, Deep & Deep Publications, New Delhi, 1993.

Chistian, Jyoti : *Class-Room Group Dynamics*, Anu Books, Meerut, 1984.

Cummings, William K., Gopinathan, S. and Tomoda, Yasumasa : *The Revival of Values Education in Asia and the West*, Pergomon Press Ple, England.

Daftrari, K.L. : *The Social Instutions in Ancient India*, Nagpur, 1947.

Das Ras Vihari, U. : *The Humanism and Education in East and West*, An International Round Table Discussion organised by UNESCO.

Di Bona, Joseph : *Critical Perspectives on Indian Education*, Bahri Publications, New Delhi, 1989.

Das, Santosh Kumar : *The Educational System of the Ancient Hindus*, Calcutta, 1930.

Deenammal, O. : *Ideology and Education*, Andhra University Press & Publications, Waltair, India, 1982.

Durkheim, Emile : *Moral Education, A Study in the theory and Application of the Sociology of Education*, The Free Press of Glencoe, Inc., U.S.A. 1925.

Dubey, R.K. : *Toward Democracy and Change in Education, Chugh Publication*, Allahabad, 1980.

Duttatreyulu, K. : *Proceedings of the Collegiate Education Conference and Seminars*, Dec. 19-21 1964, Hyderabad.

Francis, K. : *Education and Development, Social Context of Educational Development*, Vol.4, Discovery Publishing House, New Delhi, 1993.

Gandhi, M.K. : *Basic Education*, Navajivan Publishing House, Ahmedabad, 1956.

- - : *True Education*, Navajivan Publishing House, Ahmedabad, 1962.

Gautam, G. S. : *Crisis in the Temples of Learning*, S. Chand and Co. (Pvt.) Ltd., New Delhi, 1972.

Gopala Krishnaiah, V. : *New Facets of Eastern and Western Philosophies of Education*, Andhra University Press and Publications, Visakhapatnam, 1991.

Gore, M. S. : *Indian Education Structure and Process*, Rawat Publications, Jaipur, 1994.

Harold L. Hodgkinson and Myron B. Blory, Jr. (Editors), : *Identity Crisis in Higher Education*, Jassey-Bass Inc., Publishers, San Fransisco, 1971.

Jaffreys, M.C.V. : *The Aims of Education (Glaucon)*,Pitman Publishing, London, 1972.

Jayaram, N. : *Sociology of Education in India*, Rawat Publications, Jaipur, 1990.

Joshi, Kumud Ben : *Treasury of Living Words, A Selection from the Speeches of a Governer*, Sterling Publishers Private Limited, New Delhi, 1989.

Kabir, Humayun : *Indian Philosophy of Education*, Asian Publishing House, Bombay, 1964.

-- : *Education in New Delhi*, George Allen and Unwin Ltd., London.

Kaul, G.N. : *Values and Education in Independence India*, The Associated Publishers, Ambala Cant.

Kaul, J.N. : *Higher Education in India (1951-71), Two Decades of Planned Drift*, Indian Institute of Advanced Study, Simla, 1974.

Keay, F.E. : *Ancient Indian Education, An Inquiry into its Origin, Development and Ideas*, Cosmo Publication, New Delhi, 1980.

Khanna, C.P. : *Panorama of Education, Global Perspective*, Doaba House, New Delhi, 1992.

Kunhan Raja, C. : *Some Aspects of Education in Ancient India*, Adayar Library, Series, Madras, 1950.

Kraft, Arthur : *The Living Classroom Putting Humanistic Education into Practice*, Harper and Row Publishers, New York (C), 1975.

Lillie, William : *An Introduction to Ethics*, Allied Publishers Private Ltd., New Delhi, 1967.

Langford, Glen: *Education, Persons and Society: A Philosophical Enquiry*, Macmillan, 1985.

Lovell, K.: *An introduction to Human Development*, Macmillan and Co. Ltd., London, 1969.

Lunia, B.N.: *Evolution of Indian Culture*, Lakshmi Narayana Agarwal, Agra, 1977.

Mahajan, V.D.: *History of Medieval India*, S Chand and Company Ltd., New Delhi, 1991.

Mason E. Robert: *Moral Values and Secular Education*, Oxford Univeristy Press, London, 1950.

Mathur, S.S.: *A Sociological Approach to Indian Education*, Vinod Pustak Mandir, Agra, 1985.

Mauer J. George (Ed.): *Crisis in Campus Management, Case Studies in the Administration of Colleges and Universities*, Praeger Publishers, New York, 1976.

Mcclellan James E.: *Philosophy of Educaton*, Printice-Hall Inc., New Jersey, 1976.

Mehendiratta, R. Pradeep: *University Administration in India and the U.S.A., Approaches, Issues and Implications, A Comparative Study*, Oxford & IBH Publishing Co., New Delhi, 1984.

Mitra, Susil Kumar: *The Ethics of Hindus*, Asian Publication Services, New Delhi, 1978.

Mohanty, Jagannath: *Education in India*, Deep and Deep Publications, New Delhi, 1969.

Moore, G.E.: *Principia Ethica*, Cambridge University Press, Cambridge, 1976.

Morish, Ivar: *Education Since 1800*, George Allen & Unwin Ltd., London, 1970.

Morti More, Teter & Davies, Teen: *Behaviour Problems in Schools, An Evaluation of support centers*, Croom Helm Ltd., Kent, 1983.

Mozumdar, N.N.: *A Histroy of Education in Ancient India*, Macmillan & Co., Calcutta, 1916.

Mukherjee, Haridas and Mukherjee, Uma: *The Origins of the National Educaton Movement (1905-1910).* Jadavpur University, Calcutta, 1957.

Mukherhjee, R.K.: *Ancient Indian Education, Brahmanical and Buddhist,* Motilal Banarsidass, Delhi, 1969.

-- : *The Discussion of Values : A Unified Theory,* George Allen & Unwin Ltd., London, 1964.

Mukherjee, S.N.: *An Introduction to Indian Education,* Acharya Book Depot, Baroda, 1958.

--: *History of Education in India (Modern period),* Acharya Book Depot, Baroda, 1955.

Murty, K. S.: *Ethics, Education, Indian Unity and Culture,* Addresses in Universities from Kasi to Kashmir, 1080-89, Some excerts, Ajanta Publications, New Delhi, 1991.

Naik, J. P.: *Educational Planning in India,* Allied Publishers, Bomaby, 1965.

Naik, J. P. & Nurullah, Syed: *A Student's History of Education in India (1800-1973),* The Macmillan Company of India Limited, Delhi, 1974.

Narasimha Reddy, Kankanala: *Students, Teachers and Parents,* Ajanta Publications (India), Delhi, 1984.

Narayana Rao, S.: *Educational Psychology,* Wiley Eastern Limited, New Delhi, 1990.

NCERT: *The Curriculum for Ten Year School : A Frame Work,* New Delhi, 1990.

--: *National Curriculum for Primary and Secondary Education, A Frame Work,* New Delhi, NCERT (1985).

Nehru, J. L.: *Independence and After,* Publications Division, Govt. of India, New Delhi, 1987.

Nivedita, Sister: *Hints on National Education in India,* Udbodhan Office, Calcutta, 1950.

Pani, Ragunath: *Integral Educaton, Thought and Practice,* Ashish Publishing House, New Delhi, 1987.

Park, Joe.: *Selected Readings in the Philosophy of Education*, The Macmillan Company, New York, 1968.

Parikh, G.D.: *The Crisis in Higher Education*, Proceedings of a Seminar held in Bombay, Jan. 1972.

Perry, L.R.: *Educational Thinkers Series*, Betrand Russell, A.S. Neill, Homer Lane, W.H. Kilpatric Four Progressive Educators, Collier-Macmillan Limited, London, 1967.

Peters, R.S.: *Education and the Education of Teachers*, Routledge & Kegan Paul Ltd., London, 1967.

Ploghoft, Milton E. & Shuster, Albert H.: *Social Science Education in the Elementary School*, Charless E. Merrill Publilshing Co., A Bell & Howell Company, Columbus, Ohio, 1971.

Premi, M.K.: *Educational Planning in India (Implications of Population Trends)*, Sterling Publishers (P) Ltd., New Delhi, 1972.

Radhakrishnan, S. & Kumari Ranjana: *Impact of Education on Scheduled Caste Youth in India, A Study of Social Transformation in Bihar and Madhya Pradesh*, Radiant Publishers, New Delhi, 1989.

Rai, B. C.: *Philosophy of Education*, Prakasan Kendra, Lucknow, 1986.

Rai, B.C.: *History of Education*, Prakasan Kendra, Lucknow, 1991.

Saiyidain, K.G.: *The Faith of an Educationist—A Plea for Human Values*, Asia Publishing House, London, 1965.

Ranjit Sharma, G.: *Trends in Contemporary Indian Philosophy of Education : A Critical Evaluation*, Nirmal Publishers and Distributors, New Delhi, 1987.

Rao, R.B.: *Educational Environment in India, (A Multi-dimentional Study)* Chugh Publications, Allahabad, 1989.

Ray, Krishnalal: *Education in Medieval India*, B.R. Publishing Corporation, Delhi, 1984.

Rawat, P.L.: *History of Education*, Second edition, Ramaprasad & Sons, Agra, 1970.

Reid, Ivan: *The Sociology of School and Education*, Pontana Press, Colling Publishing Group, London, 1986.

Rudolph, Susanne Hoeber and Rudolph Lloyd I.: *Education and Politics in India : Studies in Organisation, Society and Policy*, Oxford University Press, 1972.

Sarma, Jogeswar: *Philosophy of Education in the Upanishads*, Orient Publications & Distributors, New Delhi, 1990.

Sarkar, S.C.: *Educational Ideas and Institutions in Ancient India (in 15th to 10th Century B.C.)*, Patna, 1928.

Sfaiyidain, K.G.: *Problems of Educational Reconstruction (3rd edn.)*, Asia Publishing House, Bombay, 1962.

- - : *Education, Culture and the Social Order*, Asia Publishing House, Bombay, 1963.

- - : *The Humanist Traditions in Indian Educational Thought*, Asia Publishing House, Bombay, 1966.

Sethi, J. D.: *The Crisis and Collapse of Higher Education in India*, Vikas Publishing House Pvt. Ltd., New Delhi, 1983.

Sharma, Om Prakash: *Administration of Education Boards in India*, Ashish Publishing House, New Delhi, 1991.

Sharma, S. R.: *Education in India*, Anmol Publications, New Delhi, 1990.

Sen, N.B.: *Progress of Education in Free India*, New Book Society of India, New Delhi, 1967.

- - : *Development of Education in New India*, New Book Society of India, New Delhi, 1966.

- - : *Advancement of Learning in Independent India*, being a symposium on education by some Ministier for Education, Vice-Chancellors and Heads of Various Departments in the Universities of India, New Book Society, New Delhi, 1967.

Shrimali, K.L.: *The Myth of University Autonomy and other Essays,* Kalamkar Prakashan Pvt. Ltd., New Delhi, 1980.

- - : *A Search for Values in Indian Education,* Vikas Publications, Delhi, 1971.

Singh, Amrik: *Redeeming Higher Education: Essays in Educational Policy,* Ajanta Publications, Delhi, 1985.

Singh, Amrik & Altbach, G. Philip: *The Higher Learning in India,* Vikas Publishing House Pvt. Ltd., Delhi, 1974.

Singh, Amrik & Sharma, G.D. (Ed): *Higher Education in India,* Konark Publishers Pvt. Ltd., Delhi, 1988.

Singh, Bhanu Pratap: *Aims of Education in India,* Ajanta Publications (India), New Delhi, 1990.

Singh, R.P. : *Educating the Indian Elite,* Sterling Publishers (P) Ltd., New Delhi, 1989.

——— (Ed).: *Indian Education in-Depth Studies,* Commonwealth Publishers, New Delhi, 1993.

Smith, Kerry G.: *Stress and Campus Response,* Jossey Bass Inc., San Fransisco, 1990.

Sinha, Jagannath: *A Manual of Ethics,* The Central Book Agency Publishers & Book Sellers, Calcutta.

Stroup, Herbett: *Four Religions of Asia,* Harper and Row Publishers, New York, 1968.

Smith, Philip G.: *Philosophy of Education, Introductory Studies,* Harper and Row, New York, 1995.

Taneja, V.P.: *Education Thought and Practices,* Sterling Publishers Private Ltd., New Delhi, 1976.

Titus, H.H. & Ketton, M.T.: *The Range of Ethics, Introductory Readings,* Affiliated East-West Press Pvt. Ltd., New Delhi, 1972.

Tiwari, D.D.: *Education at the Cross Roads,* Chugh Publications, Allahabad, 1975.

Vakil, K.S. and Natarajan, S.: *Edication in India* (3rd Rev. Ed.), Allied Publishers, Bombay, 1972.

Veena, D. R.: *Education System : Problems and Prospects,* Ashish Publishing House, New Delhi, 1988.

Vohra, Amrit Lal & Sharma, Sita Ram: *Management of Higher Education in India,* Anmol Publications, New Delhi, 1990.

Vyas, R.N. : *Recreating Educational system for a New World (Spiritual basis of Education),* Vohra Publishers & Distributors, Allahabad, 1986.

Wallace, G. and Walker, A.D.M. (Ed.) : *The Definition of Morality,* Mathuen & Co. Ltd., London, 1970.

Warnock, G.J. : *The Object of Morality,* Methuen & Co. Ltd., London, 1971.

Whitehead, Alfred North : *Amis of Education and Other Essays,*The Macmillan Company, New york, 1927.

JOURNALS

The Journal of Higher Education, Ohio State University Press, American Association for Higher Education.

(The) Educational Review, a monthly record for India, The Educational Review, Triplicane, Madras (India), from 1985 to 1996.

Journal of Indian Education, NCERT, from 1978 to 1995.

Daily News Papers

The Hindu

Times of India

Hindustan Times

Index